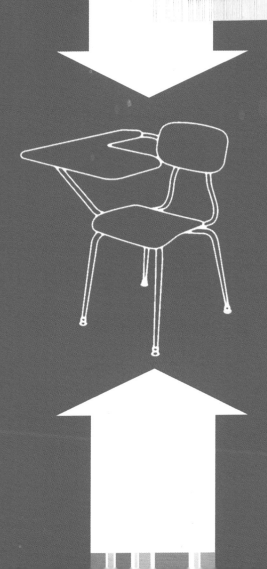

YEAR:	NAME:	CONDITION:

0-7607-6279-1

Published exclusively for Barnes & Noble, Inc., by Gusto Company.

© 2004 GUSTO Company As

Written by Michael Powell

Illustrations by Allen Boe and AnnDréa Boe

Executive Editor and original concept by James Tavendale

Edited by Katherine Robinson and Rachel Elliot

Designed by Allen Boe

STUFF YOU SHOULD HAVE LEARNED AT SCHOOL

By Michael Powell

BARNES
& NOBLE
BOOKS
NEW YORK

INTRODUCTION

If your schooldays were the happiest days of your life, you either had a great time and learned nothing or you've had a miserable existence ever since. Maybe you were the kind of pupil who, when asked to explain the theory of gravity, threw your teacher out of the window.

Can you name 10 United States presidents or explain plate tectonics to your granny? Do you know who invented the Post-It note and how to add fractions? Have you ever attempted to read James Joyce's *Ulysses*?

That's why this little book shouldn't ever leave your backpack (can't bear to throw it away, huh?). It's packed with all that stuff that you should have learned at school when you were too busy with . . . um . . . other stuff.

Here's your chance to bone up on 50 of the big ideas you might have heard of if you hadn't been screwing off, smoking behind the bike racks, sleeping, or just being plain stupid. It wouldn't kill you to have a second chance, would it?

So eyes on the blackboard and pay attention!

"Outside of a dog, a book is a man's best friend and inside of a dog, it's too dark to read."

— Groucho Marx

ENGLISH

Literary Criticism and Theory

Literary criticism is the interpretation and evaluation of the literary qualities of a text with reference to personal and cultural significance, the use of language, and the aesthetic effect, and placing the text within the context of genres and literature as a whole. Literary theory examines the nature of literature itself (asking questions such as "What is literature?") and its purpose and functions, and attempts to understand the frames of reference applied to judgments of literature.

Different schools, or types, of literary theory and criticism take individual approaches to understanding texts. Here are the broad schools that have been most influential during the last century.

New Criticism:

New Criticism started in the late 1920s and proposed that a work should be judged and interpreted by detailed reference to the text alone; it should be treated as an autonomous entity, separate from other factors such as the author's biographical details or "intended meaning." This approach opens up the text to rich "ambiguity" and many simultaneous meanings.

Archetypal/Myth Criticism:

Archetypal, or Myth, Criticism involves viewing the text and its genre, plots, and characters in terms of recurrent archetypes or mythic patterns that Carl Jung described as "primordial images," a common language of symbols that is passed down from generation to generation, inherited in our "collective unconscious." It treats literature as an active process that involves the reader at a deep psychological level because he or she brings experience of these symbols to a reading of the text.

Psychoanalytic Criticism:

Psychoanalytic Criticism applies modern psychological ideas (particularly those of Sigmund Freud) to the study of literature and often uses them to psychoanalyze the author. This literary movement also applies psychological principles to interpret the motivations and conflicts of the characters.

Marxist Criticism:

Marxist Criticism is based on the philosophical, political, and economic theories of Karl Marx and Friedrich Engels, who believed that "it is not the consciousness of men that determines their existence . . . but their social existence that determines their consciousness." Therefore, Marxist critics always interpret the form and content of a text in the context of the historical, economic, and sociological forces that shaped it.

Karl Marx

Russian Formalism:

Russian Formalism, a diverse linguistic movement that began in the 1920s, viewed literature as being composed of an autonomous, largely self-referential language, a sum of literary and artistic devices, as distinct from ordinary spoken language, which is largely functional. Its focus is to define and analyze the unique features and functions of this formal "poetic language."

Structuralism:

Structuralism is a way of viewing the world (and literature) that places more importance on the structures that link individual elements than the elements themselves, which have no intrinsic importance or even existence in isolation. Everything in the world is textual in the sense that it is composed of signs and ordered according to a pattern of relationships. This approach has helped take literature off its pedestal and allowed a wider study of "textuality" in more "popularist" forms of writing.

Post-Structuralism and Deconstruction:

Post-Structuralism and Deconstruction was a reaction to Structuralism. It aimed to view a text as having no knowable center or meaning but an infinite set of meanings, rendering any attempt to take meaning from the structure as futile and, in fact, meaningless. It can also be crudely summed up as "death to the author"— the idea that once a text has been written, it ceases to be the domain of the author and cannot be read as communicating a single message, but will present many coexisting and conflicting with each other. This school of thought also tries to demonstrate that binary ideas, such as maleness and femaleness, or good and evil, are not polar but fluid and exist on a continuum.

Feminist Criticism:

Put very simply, Feminist Criticism aims to reinterpret language and literature, which has for so long been dominated by male beliefs and preoccupations. It explores the relationship between writing and gender; rediscovers, re-examines, and reprints women's literature of the past; seeks to challenge and raise awareness of male and female stereotypes and sexist and patriarchal attitudes in literature; defines recurrent feminist themes and develops a new feminist writing.

Reader-Response Theory:

Reader-Response Theory suggests that the reader produces his or her own highly subjective meanings. This broad approach can accommodate, at one end of the spectrum, the—some would say elitist—idea that there is a "correct" reading that the "educated" reader can attain by developing a sophisticated interpretive strategy. But it can also allow a relativistic analysis that the reader actually creates the text.

Literary Forms and Terms

Do you know the difference between a trochee and an iambic pentameter, or a simile and a metaphor? Here is all you need to know to cut it in the big bad world of literature.

Alexandrine: a line of verse that has six iambic feet

Allegory: a story, poem, or play in which the events and characters have symbolic meanings beyond their literal sense

Alliteration: the repetition of the same consonants (usually initial ones) or stressed syllables (e.g., "Around the rocks the rugged rascal ran.")

Anapaest: a metrical foot with three syllables, the first two unstressed and the last stressed: "di-di-<u>dum</u>"

Assonance: the repetition of identical or similar vowel sounds (e.g., "all for naught")

Blank Verse: unrhymed verse (often iambic pentameter). Frequently used by Shakespeare (see page 16)

Couplet: a pair of successive lines of poetry, usually rhyming and with the same meter. Made popular by Chaucer (see page 14)

Dactyl: a metrical foot with three syllables, the first stressed and the last two unstressed: "<u>dum</u>-di-di"

Dramatic Irony: in a work of fiction (usually a play) when the audience knows something important that the character does not

Foot: the basic unit or metrical division for verse, made up of two or more syllables —iamb, trochee, spondee, anapaest, dactyl

Feminine Rhyme: a rhyme of two syllables with the final syllable unstressed (e.g., "people/steeple")

Homophones: words with different meanings but exactly the same sound (e.g., whether/weather; reel/real)

Hyberbole: deliberate exaggeration for effect (e.g., "I've told you a thousand times," "I could eat a horse")

Iamb: a metrical foot with two syllables, the first unstressed and the second stressed: "di-<u>dum</u>"

Iambic Pentameter: a line of verse with five iambic feet: "di-<u>dum</u> di-<u>dum</u> di-<u>dum</u> di-<u>dum</u> di-<u>dum</u>"

Masculine Rhyme: a rhyme of one syllable, or two stressed final syllables, with the first syllable unstressed (e.g., "delay/today")

Metaphor: a figure of speech in which a word or phrase is used to designate another (e.g., "Money is a monster," "This place is a pig sty.")

Metonym: a figure of speech in which the name of one object is replaced by another word that is closely associated with it (e.g., "plastic" for "credit card," "Washington" for "United States government")

Meter: the pattern of stresses in a line of poetry; a rhythmic arrangement of syllables

Onomatopoeia: using words which sound like the sounds they are describing (e.g., "crunch," "crackle," "cuckoo")

Oxymoron: a figure of speech that combines two contradictory terms (e.g., "deafening silence," "honest liar," "terribly good")

Simile: a figure of speech that associates two words or phrases through comparison, using "as" or "like" (e.g., "This place is like a pig sty," "She is as quiet as a mouse.")

Sonnet: a poem with 14 lines, usually in iambic pentameter

Spondee: a metrical foot with two long or stressed syllables: "<u>dum</u>-<u>dum</u>" (e.g., "pancake," "blackbird")

Stanza: a group of two or more lines in a poem, usually with a common pattern of meter and rhyme

Trochee: a metrical foot with two syllables, the first stressed, the second unstressed: "<u>dum</u>-di" (e.g., "broken," "talking")

Geoffrey Chaucer

Apart from William Shakespeare, the poet Geoffrey Chaucer (born c.1343) is probably the most significant writer in the English language. He was one of the first people to write in English, which was considered an inferior language for literature at the time (Latin and French were more acceptable).

Nevertheless, Chaucer's readers would not have been commoners, since only noblemen were literate. He was the son of a wealthy vintner, who was also a diplomat and yeoman of the king. He was well educated and probably fluent in several languages, including French, Italian, and Latin.

His early works included the "Parlement of Foules," a 700-line allegorical love poem about a bunch of talking birds, and an 8,000-line love poem, "Troilus and Criseyde," about a Trojan prince and a priest's daughter set against a backdrop of the Trojan War.

His master work was *The Canterbury Tales*, a landmark of English literature. It's a collection of 24 stories told by a fictional group of 30 pilgrims on their way to Canterbury (Chaucer didn't finish the manuscript). They meet at the Tabard Inn in London and decide to have a story-telling competition on their journey. The characters come from a wide cross-section of society, from the bawdy Wife of Bath to the romantic Knight, and the types of stories and the language used vividly reflect the pretensions, character, and preoccupations of the individual pilgrims, and give us a glimpse into life in the Middle Ages.

Chaucer's diplomatic travels took him to Italy, so he probably copied the idea for the structure of the tales from Boccaccio's *Decameron* in which 10 nobles tell each other stories in a country villa outside Florence.

He was a funny writer. Here's one of his best gags from "The Miller's Tale," a medieval romp about adultery, lust, and deceit.

And up the wyndowe dide he hastily,
And out his ers he putteth pryvely.

(Nicholas, the lodger, sticks his bottom out of the window, pretending to be the wife of an old man whose wife he wants to bed.)

This Nicholas anon leet fle a fart,
As greet as it had been a thonder-dent,

(Nicholas lets fly a fart like a thunder clap.)

And he was redy with his iren hoot,
And nicholas amydde the ers he smoot.

(Instead of kissing Nicholas, his rival Absolon sticks a red hot poker up his bottom.)

The Chopping Bard: Ten Shakespeare Plays

It is generally accepted that William Shakespeare (1564–1616) wrote or collaborated on at least 37 plays, but he wrote far more comedies than anything else. He penned 17 comedies, 10 histories, and 10 tragedies. Here are the zip files for 10 of his masterpieces.

Romeo and Juliet:

Star-crossed teenagers Romeo and Juliet fall in love and marry in secret because their families, the Montagues and the Capulets, hate each other's guts. Romeo is banished after killing Juliet's cousin Tybalt in a fight, so he and Juliet have sex and he leaves the next morning. Juliet's dad wants her to marry someone else, so she drinks a potion to make her seem dead. Romeo thinks she's really dead and kills himself. Juliet wakes up, discovers Romeo dead, and kills herself, too.

Macbeth:

Macbeth and his friend Banquo run into three witches who predict Macbeth will be Thane of Cawdor, and then king. They also predict that Banquo will beget kings, but not be one. After Macbeth's pushy wife persuades him to kill King Duncan, he becomes king and has Banquo killed. Then, after he is haunted by guilt and Banquo's ghost, the witches tell him to beware of Macduff, that no one born of a woman can harm him, and that he will be okay so long as Birnam Wood doesn't come to his castle. So he has Macduff's wife and children killed. Lady Macbeth goes mad and dies, and Duncan's son Malcolm leads an army that camouflages itself in branches cut from Birnam Wood. They come to Macbeth's castle where Macduff (who, it turns out, was delivered by Caesarian section) kills him. Malcolm becomes king.

The Tempest:

Exiled by his brother Antonio, former king Prospero has been living on a remote island with his daughter Miranda for 12 years when the play begins. Skilled in magic, he has the spirit Ariel at his command. Prospero conjures a storm to shipwreck Antonio and others on the island, where

Miranda falls in love with Ferdinand. Prospero's monster slave, Caliban, plots to kill his master with Stefano, but fails. Prospero forgives his brother on the condition that he regains the throne. Prospero then liberates Ariel and they all abandon Caliban on the island.

Hamlet:

Prince Hamlet's dad is murdered by his uncle, Claudius, who marries his mom, Gertrude, and takes the throne. Hamlet is told by his dad's ghost to avenge the murder, but spends most of the play dithering and feeling depressed ("To be or not to be . . .") until finally he arranges for a touring theater company to perform a play re-enacting the murder to expose Claudius. Feigning madness, Hamlet snubs his girlfriend Ophelia ("Get thee to a nunnery..."), shouts at his mom, and then unintentionally stabs and kills Ophelia's dad, who is hiding behind a curtain. Ophelia goes mad and drowns herself in a brook. Hamlet has a sword fight with her avenging brother Laertes and they both die from a poisoned foil, but not before Gertrude has swallowed a poisoned drink meant for him and Hamlet has killed Claudius.

Othello:

The daughter of a Venetian senator controversially marries Othello, a Moor in the service of the state. His soldier friend Iago, resentful of being passed over for a promotion, convinces Othello that his wife Desdemona has been unfaithful with Cassio. Othello smothers Desdemona, discovers he was wrong, Iago is arrested, and Othello kills himself.

A Midsummer Night's Dream:

Hermia loves Lysander but is supposed to marry Demetrius, whom Helena loves. Hermia's dad gives her four days to agree or else die or become a nun. The four lovers get lost in the woods where the fairy king Oberon and his mischievous sprite Puck mess with everyone's heads. Much hilarity ensues after Puck's spell goes wrong and the four lovers pair off with the wrong people and the fairy queen Titania falls for a weaver called Bottom whom Puck has given a donkey's head. It all gets sorted out in the end, Hermia is forgiven, and everyone marries their true love and lives happily ever after.

The Merchant of Venice:

Bassanio borrows money from his merchant mate, Antonio, so he can wed Portia. Because Antonio's money is tied up with foreign trade, Antonio in turn borrows the money from a Jewish usurer called Shylock on condition that if Antonio doesn't repay the money he will forfeit a pound of flesh. When Antonio can't pay up, Shylock demands his pound of flesh. So Portia dresses up as a judge and rules that Shylock can take it, so long as he doesn't draw any blood. Since this is impossible, he must be also be guilty of attempted murder and forfeits half his wealth and has to convert to Christianity and be reconciled with his daughter whom he had previously disinherited for marrying a Christian.

Julius Caesar:

Despite his wife Calpurnia's bad dreams and a warning to "Beware the Ides of March," Caesar goes to the Senate and is murdered by Cassius and Casca who didn't want him to be crowned king. They had also persuaded the noble Brutus to join in ("Et tu, Brute?"). At Caesar's funeral, Antony stirs up the crowd against the conspirators ("Friends, Romans, countrymen, lend me your ears") and then, with Octavius and Lepidus, defeats them at the battle of Philippi. Brutus' wife dies tragically, and Brutus (the only honorable guy in the whole play) and Cassius commit suicide.

King Lear:

King Lear asks his three daughters, Goneril, Regan, and Cordelia, which one loves him the most. The first two sisters flatter him rotten, but Cordelia says she loves him only according to her duty. Lear is furious and disinherits her, then announces he will stay with a 100 knights at each daughter's home in turn. Goneril and Regan begrudge the visit and turn him out in a storm. The Earl of Gloucester shows pity for Lear, but he has his eyes put out by Regan's husband. Gloucester's son Edgar, disguised as a beggar, looks after Lear. Finally Lear goes mad and Cordelia dutifully looks after him. Goneril and Regan both fancy Gloucester's bastard son Edmund, so Goneril poisons Regan, then commits suicide. Edmund has Cordelia hanged, Lear dies from grief, Edmund is exposed by Edgar, then Goneril's husband becomes king.

Richard III:

Deformed Richard of Gloucester wants to become king and sets out to remove any competition. He has his brother, the Duke of Clarence, murdered and marries Anne after chatting her up at her dad's funeral. He kills some more people and is crowned king before murdering his nephews Edward V and Richard Duke of York (the princes in the Tower). Richard tries to marry his niece, Elizabeth of York, after the death of his wife Anne (a death that he encouraged), but he is defeated by Henry Tudor's army at the Battle of Bosworth after he loses his horse ("A horse, a horse, my kingdom for a horse. . ."). Henry Tudor, Earl of Richmond, becomes King Henry VII, founding the Tudor dynasty.

Goethe

Poet, playwright, novelist, scientist, and natural philosopher, Goethe is Germany's greatest writer and a giant of Western literature. During his lifetime, German culture enjoyed a golden age of literary movements: Storm and Stress (Sturm und Drang), Classicism (Klassik), and Romanticism (Romantik), but only Goethe, ever evolving and developing, managed to span all three. The period of 1770–1832 is even known as "The Age of Goethe."

"You must be either the master or the servant, the hammer or the anvil."

Goethe was born in 1749 in Frankfurt and was a precocious youngster, who by the age of eight had a good grasp of Greek, Latin, French, and Italian. He later described his happy sheltered childhood in his autobiography, *Poetry and Truth*. In 1765 he studied law in Leipzig and later at Strasbourg, where he was introduced to Gothic architecture, Homer, Shakespeare, folk poetry, and Germany's medieval past. Other major influences of his youth were J.-J. Rousseau and Spinoza, who tapped into Goethe's mystic affinity with nature. He also began a lifelong passion for the study of plants and animals.

After falling in love with a pastor's daughter, Friederike Brion, he produced some of his finest lyrical poems, which earned him recognition, but his first major work was a protest drama, *Götz von Berlichingen* (1773). This was followed by *Die Leiden des jungen Werthers* (The Sorrows of Young Werther), which he wrote in a suicidal depression after being spurned by Charlotte Buff. The book created a sensation and brought him widespread fame; it even inspired a series of youthful suicides throughout Europe (Werther takes his own life at the end).

In 1775 he was invited to the court at Saxe-Weimar, where he spent the rest of his life and held a succession of political offices; for 10 years he was chief minister of state. By 1786, drained by a long love affair with Charlotte von Stein, he traveled in Italy (described in *Italian Journey*), where he immersed himself in classical antiquity and explored the ideas of "noble simplicity and quiet grandeur," writing *Egmont, Roman Elegies, Torquato Tasso, Hermann and Dorothea,* and *Iphigenia in Tauris*. He also continued his scientific research, which in many ways was more important to him than his writing—he even inspired Charles Darwin with his discovery of the human premaxilla jaw bones.

In 1794 he formed a friendship with the poet and dramatist Friedrich Schiller, a relationship that grew to have a profound influence on his writing. After Schiller's death, Goethe published the first part of *Faust*, one of the peaks of his achievements (the second part was published posthumously), and wrote one of his most important novels, *Elective Affinities*.

Goethe's literary canon has been translated, imitated, and set to music by many of the major literary and artistic figures who succeeded him. There are 2,660 musical compositions alone based on his works; his philosophy shaped two centuries of thinking and championed the organic and evolving expression of the individual. His legacy is some of the most personal, intuitive, and finely crafted poetic and philosophic writing the world has ever seen.

Fifty-Four Great Poets

Here is a list of some of the greatest Western poets and a few of their poems or books to get you started.

Maya Angelou (b. 1928):
"Just Give Me a Cool Drink of Water 'Fore I Diiie"

W. H. Auden (1907–1973):
"Spain," "Funeral Blues," "For the Time Being"

John Berryman (1914–1972):
The Dream Songs

William Blake (1757–1827):
Songs of Innocence, Songs of Experience, The Marriage of Heaven and Hell

Robert Bridges (1844–1930):
"Awake, My Heart," "Nightingales"

Rupert Brooke (1887–1915):
The War Sonnets: "Peace," "Safety," "The Dead," "The Soldier"

Elizabeth Barrett Browning (1806–1861):
"Sonnets from the Portuguese," *Aurora Leigh*

Robert Browning (1812–1889):
Men and Women, "My Last Duchess," "The Boy and the Angel"

Robert Burns (1759–1796):
"A Red, Red Rose," "Scots Wha Hae"

John Clare (1793–1864):
"Remembrances," "The Flitting," "Decay"

Samuel Taylor Coleridge (1772–1834):
"The Rime of the Ancient Mariner," "Kubla Khan," "This Lime-Tree Bower My Prison," "Frost at Midnight," "Dejection: An Ode," "The Pains of Sleep"

e. e. cummings (1894–1962):
Complete Poems, 1904–1962, who knows if the moon's, lily has a rose, in a middle of a room

Emily Dickinson (1830–1886):
"There came a wind like a bugle," "As imperceptibly as Grief"

John Donne (1572–1631):
"The Flea," "The Sonne Rising,"
"The Anniversarie," "A Valediction:
Forbidding Mourning"

John Dryden (1631–1700):
"Absalom and Achitophel," "Annus
Mirabilis," "MacFlecknoe"

Paul Laurence Dunbar (1872–1906):
Lyrics of Lowly Life

T. S. Eliot (1888–1965):
"The Waste Land"

Robert Frost (1874–1963):
"The Road Not Taken," "Acquainted With
the Night," "Stopping By Woods On a
Snowy Evening"

Allen Ginsberg (1926–1997):
Howl and Other Poems

Thomas Hardy (1840–1928):
"Ah, Are You Digging On My Grave?,"
"The Man He Killed"

Tony Harrison (b. 1937):
"V. "

Seamus Heaney (b. 1939):
"Digging," "Personal Helicon," "Casualty"

George Herbert (1593–1633):
"The Collar," "Love," "The Pearl"

Oliver Wendell Holmes (1809–1894):
"Old Ironsides"

Gerard Manley Hopkins (1844–1889):
"The Wreck of the Deutschland,"
"God's Grandeur," "As Kingfishers Catch
Fire," "Pied Beauty," "Carrion Comfort,"
"The Windhover: To Christ Our Lord"

Ted Hughes (1930–1998):
The Hawk in the Rain, "The Thought-Fox,"
"Crow's Nerve Fails"

James Weldon Johnson (1871–1938):
God's Trombones

John Keats (1795–1821):
"Endymion: A Poetic Romance," "La Belle
Dame Sans Merci," "Ode to Psyche," "Ode
on a Grecian Urn," "Ode to a Nightingale,"
"To Autumn"

Jack Kerouac (1922–1969):
Scattered Poems, Book of Haikus,
"How To Meditate"

Philip Larkin (1922–1985):
"Ambulances," "Annus Mirabilis,"
"Church Going," "The Whitsun Weddings,"
"This Be the Verse"

**Henry Wadsworth Longfellow
(1807–1882):**
The Song of Hiawatha

Amy Lowell (1874–1925):
"The Garden by the Moonlight," "Autumn,"
"In Excelsis"

Archibald MacLeish (1892–1982):
"You, Andrew Marvell," "Dr. Sigmund
Freud Discovers the Sea Shell," "The wild
old wicked man"

John Masefield (1878–1967):
"Sea Fever," "Cargoes,"
"Christmas Eve at Sea"

John Milton (1608–1674):
Paradise Lost

Wilfred Owen (1893–1918):
"Anthem for Doomed Youth," "Dulce
et Decorum Est," "The Parable of the
Old Man and the Young"

Dorothy Parker (1893–1967):
"Resumé," "One Perfect Rose,"
"Unfortunate Coincidence"

Sylvia Plath (1932–1963):
Ariel, The Collected Poems

Alexander Pope (1688–1744):
"The Rape of the Lock,"
"Windsor Forest," "Dunciad"

Ezra Pound (1885–1972):
The Cantos

Adrienne Rich (b. 1929):
Diving into the Wreck

**Edwin Arlington Robinson
(1869–1935):**
"Luke Havergal," "The House on the Hill,"
"John Evereldown"

Theodore Roethke (1908–1963):
"The Waking"

Christina Rossetti (1830–1894):
"The Lambs of Grasmere, 1860,"
"Symbols," "Remember," "A Birthday"

Siegfried Sassoon (1886–1967):
"They," "The Hero," "Base Details,"
"Glory of Women"

Anne Sexton (1928–1974):
Love Poems

Percy Bysshe Shelley (1792–1822):
Queen Mab: A Philosophical Poem,
"Alastor: or, the Spirit of Solitude," "Hymn
to Intellectual Beauty," "Mont Blanc," "The
Masque of Anarchy," "Song-To the Men of
England," "To a Skylark," "The Cloud,"
"Ode to the West Wind"

Edmund Spenser (1552–1599):
The Faerie Queene, "Epithalamion"

Wallace Stevens (1879–1955):
"The Man with the Blue Guitar," "The
Emperor of Ice-Cream," "Peter Quince at
the Clavier," "The Idea of Order at Key West"

Alfred Tennyson (1809–1892):
"The Charge of the Light Brigade,"
"The Lady of Shalott," "The Lotos-Eaters,"
"Crossing the Bar," "St. Agnes' Eve"

Dylan Thomas (1914–1953):
"Do Not Go Gentle into That Good Night,"
"Fern Hill"

Walt Whitman (1819–1892):
Leaves of Grass

William Carlos Williams (1883–1963):
Paterson

William Butler Yeats (1865–1939):
"Falling of Leaves," "When You Are
Old," "The Lake Isle of Innisfree,"
"The Second Coming," "The Tower,"
"Sailing to Byzantium"

Dylan Thomas

One Hundred Must-Read Novels

If you feel that you don't read enough (who doesn't?), but you don't know where to start, here are 100 of the best books ever written. If you read one each week, within two years you'll know more about literature than most college graduates. If you start reading one of these books and aren't enjoying it, try another one and come back to it later. If nothing else, reading should be fun, at best totally absorbing.

1. *1984* by George Orwell
2. *Absalom, Absalom!* by William Faulkner
3. *The Adventures of Augie March* by Saul Bellow
4. *The Adventures of Huckleberry Finn* by Mark Twain
5. *The Age of Innocence* by Edith Wharton
6. *The Alexandria Quartet* by Lawrence Durrell
7. *All the King's Men* by Robert Penn Warren
8. *The Ambassadors* by Henry James
9. *An American Tragedy* by Theodore Dreiser
10. *Angle of Repose* by Wallace Stegner
11. *Anna Karenina* by Leo Tolstoy
12. *Appointment in Samarra* by John O'Hara
13. *As I Lay Dying* by William Faulkner
14. *A Bend in the River* by V.S. Naipaul
15. *Brave New World* by Aldous Huxley
16. *The Bridge of San Luis Rey* by Thornton Wilder
17. *The Brothers Karamazov* by Fyodor M. Dostoyevsky
18. *The Call of the Wild* by Jack London
19. *Catch-22* by Joseph Heller
20. *The Catcher in the Rye* by J. D. Salinger
21. *A Clockwork Orange* by Anthony Burgess
22. *Darkness at Noon* by Arthur Koestler
23. *The Day of the Locust* by Nathanael West
24. *Death Comes for the Archbishop* by Willa Cather
25. *The Death of the Heart* by Elizabeth Bowen
26. *Deliverance* by James Dickey
27. *Don Quixote* by Miguel de Cervantes
28. *A Farewell to Arms* by Ernest Hemingway
29. *From Here to Eternity* by James Jones
30. *Go Tell It on the Mountain* by James Baldwin
31. *The Golden Bowl* by Henry James
32. *The Good Soldier* by Ford Madox Ford
33. *The Grapes of Wrath* by John Steinbeck
34. *The Great Gatsby* by F. Scott Fitzgerald

35. *A Handful of Dust* by Evelyn Waugh

36. *The Heart Is a Lonely Hunter* by Carson McCullers

37. *Heart of Darkness* by Joseph Conrad

38. *The Heart of the Matter* by Graham Greene

39. *Henderson the Rain King* by Saul Bellow

40. *A High Wind in Jamaica* by Richard Hughes

41. *A House for Mr. Biswas* by V. S. Naipaul

42. *The House of Mirth* by Edith Wharton

43. *Howards End* by E. M. Forster

44. *Invisible Man* by Ralph Ellison

45. *Ironweed* by William Kennedy

46. *Jane Eyre* by Charlotte Brontë

47. *Kim* by Rudyard Kipling

48. *Light in August* by William Faulkner

49. *Lord Jim* by Joseph Conrad

50. *Lord of the Flies* by William Golding

51. *Loving* by Henry Green

52. *The Magus* by John Fowles

53. *Main Street* by Sinclair Lewis

54. *The Maltese Falcon* by Dashiell Hammett

55. *Midnight's Children* by Salman Rushdie

56. *The Moviegoer* by Walker Percy

57. *The Naked and the Dead* by Norman Mailer

58. *Native Son* by Richard Wright

59. *Nostromo* by Joseph Conrad

60. *Of Human Bondage* by W. Somerset Maugham

61. *The Old Wives' Tale* by Arnold Bennett

62. *On the Road* by Jack Kerouac

63. *One Flew Over the Cuckoo's Nest* by Ken Kesey

64. *Pale Fire* by Vladimir Nabokov

65. *Parade's End* by Ford Madox Ford

66. *A Passage to India* by E. M. Forster

67. *The Picture of Dorian Gray* by Oscar Wilde

68. *Point Counter Point* by Aldous Huxley

69. *A Portrait of the Artist as a Young Man* by James Joyce

70. *A Prayer for Owen Meany* by John Irving

71. *Pride and Prejudice* by Jane Austen

72. *The Prime of Miss Jean Brodie* by Muriel Spark

73. *Ragtime* by E. L. Doctorow

74. *The Rainbow* by D. H. Lawrence

75. *A Room With a View* by E. M. Forster

76. *Scoop* by Evelyn Waugh

77. *The Secret Agent* by Joseph Conrad

78. *The Sheltering Sky* by Paul Bowles

79. *Sister Carrie* by Theodore Dreiser

80. *Slaughterhouse-Five* by Kurt Vonnegut

81. *Sons and Lovers* by D. H. Lawrence

82. *The Sound and the Fury* by William Faulkner

83. *The Stranger* by Albert Camus

84. *Studs Lonigan: A Trilogy* by James T. Farrell

85. *The Sun Also Rises* by Ernest Hemingway

86. *Tender Is the Night* by F. Scott Fitzgerald

87. *Things Fall Apart* by Chinua Achebe

88. *The Tin Drum* by Günter Grass

89. *To Kill a Mockingbird* by Harper Lee

90. *To the Lighthouse* by Virginia Woolf

91. *Tobacco Road* by Erskine Caldwell

92. *Tropic of Cancer* by Henry Miller

93. *Ulysses* by James Joyce

94. *Under the Net* by Iris Murdoch

95. *Under the Volcano* by Malcolm Lowry

96. *The Wapshot Chronicle* by John Cheever

97. *The Way of All Flesh* by Samuel Butler

98. *The Wings of the Dove* by Henry James

99. *Women in Love* by D.H. Lawrence

100. *Wuthering Heights* by Emily Brontë

Ten Spelling Tips

1

Use I before E except after C;
When A or I is the sound,
It's the other way round

As in the following examples:
CEI: ceiling, receipt, deceive
IE: yield, relieve, belief
EI: freight, reign, vein

Some exceptions: foreign, heir, weird, either, heifer, leisure, and seismic.
Another exception is the "CIEN" formations such as ancient, deficient, and science.

2

"When two vowels go walking, the first one does the talking." When there are two vowels in a row, the first is the one you hear, as in stream, boat, and death.

3

Break complicated words into syllables and compare the components to other words with which you are familiar.

4

Use mnemonics and memory tricks to help you distinguish between two similar words. For example, stationery and stationary—there is an e (for envelope) in stationery
   desperate era (i.e., there is an era in desperate)
   occasion to see (i.e., there are two Cs—"occasion to s" doesn't make sense!)
   necessary = 1 collar (1 C) — 2 socks (2 Ss)

5

Try to develop an intuitive sense of when a word looks wrong. You might not know what is wrong, but it's the first step in correcting your mistake.

6

Make a list of your most common spelling mistakes—and learn the correct spellings. It's never too late. Most of us have words that we consistently spell incorrectly, but you won't improve if you can't remember which they are.

7

Plurals.
Most words ending in "s," "ss," "sh," "ch," "x," or "zz," add "es" in the plural.
Most words ending in "o" add "s" in the plural (e.g., hero, potato, tomato).
Most words ending in "f" become "ves" in the plural (e.g., elf, wolf, and shelf, but not roof, dwarf, and chief).

8

The only word that ends in "full" is the word "full"—all the rest end in "ful."

9

Hyphens: If in doubt, leave it out. Spell most compound nouns as one word.

10

There are only three two-syllable words that end in "eed": exceed, proceed, and succeed. All the rest are "ede": precede, recede, concede, intercede.

Ten Grammar Tips

1 "It's" with an apostrophe is the contraction of "it is" or "it has."
Possessive uses do not use an apostrophe.

For example, "It's hot today." "It's raining." "It's been raining." "Its meaning should be obvious!"

However, an apostrophe indicates possessive in a singular noun and comes before the "s": *The horse's stable; the train's departure*

In the plural it comes after the "s": *The horses' stable (there is more than one horse).*

2 The verb to "accept" is used in connection with receiving something; the verb to "except" means to exclude or omit.

He accepted money from me.

An admission fee is charged, but guests are excepted.

3 I *lie* there every day. (He *lies* there.)
I *lay* there yesterday.
I *will lie* there next week.
I *am lying* there now.
I *have lain* there every week since Christmas.

4 Only use "whom" for an object, not a subject:

You will send this letter to the person who appears on the envelope.

We were sued by the employee whom we fired last year.

Whom are you calling?

5 Use "fewer" for quantities that can be counted and "less" for those which cannot.

Today you have eaten fewer donuts than yesterday.

My shirt contains less mud than yours.

(Remember "mud" to prove the rule since "fewer mud" is clearly wrong)

My shirt contains fewer patches of mud than yours.

(Patches of mud can be counted—if you can be bothered!)

Your book has fewer pages than mine. *(Pages can be counted)*

Do not use commas to bracket phrases that are essential to a sentence's meaning.

6

INCORRECT: The horse, with the lightest rider, stands the best chance of winning this race.
CORRECT: The horse with the lightest rider stands the best chance of winning this race.

Ensure the subject and verb agree with each other, not with a word or phrase that comes between them.

7

The man, together with his seven wives, was walking along the road.
The building, along with its ornate entrance and staircase, was the subject of much media interest.

Use the active voice in preference to the passive voice.

8

WEAK: A present was given to her when she left the company.
BETTER: The company gave her a present when she left.

WEAK: A check and a letter of commendation were presented to the winner by the managing director.
BETTER: The managing director presented a check and a letter of commendation to the winner.

Don't confuse "complement" with "compliment."

9

Complement (verb or noun) implies something that completes, makes up a whole, or brings to perfection.
Compliment (verb or noun) implies an expression of praise, admiration, or congratulation.

Unique means, "being the only one of its kind." It is absolute, so something can't be "very unique," "more unique," or "less unique," just as one can't be "very dead," "more dead," or "less dead."

10

James Joyce and *Ulysses*

Ulysses, a Modernist reconstruction of Homer's epic the *Odyssey* (see page 114), is arguably the greatest literary achievement of the twentieth century. It is, without question, a work of genius.

Published in 1922, it was banned in the United Kingdom and the United States for its "pornographic" content; it was the standard bearer of the Modernist movement; it has been criticized by literary giants such as Virginia Woolf and generations of readers since for its opacity. It weaves together symbolism, philosophy, religion, politics, and social realism, and reinvents the written form; it can never be fully grasped or exhausted. It is a controversial masterpiece whose integrity is still the stuff of contentious court cases—the Joyce estate fiercely protects every word and punctuation mark from "revisionist" editors.

However, to the common reader, *Ulysses* is, without doubt, one of the most "difficult" books in the universe. But it is this undoubted complexity that highlights one of the greatest questions in literature—the subjective nature of the literary experience.

Joyce was writing for a general readership. One of the contradictions of a great work is that it can do two apparently contradictory things at the same time—namely *Ulysses* does more to knock "literature" off its pedestal than any novel written before or since, while at the same time being so densely layered and original that most people are scared away. That said, a beach read it is not.

There is enough secondary literature on Joyce elsewhere in the world to make any attempted paraphrase of the themes, plot, and language of *Ulysses* trivial, alienating, and counterproductive. It is included in this book because, since participation is more important than understanding, you should read *Ulysses* and get from it what you will. Also it is a good touch paper for the issues raised in the Literary Theory section (see page 8).

If you hate it, read something else. Come back to it later, perhaps. But above all, don't let anyone tell you that you're not smart enough to "get it."

What you should have learned at school is that literature is fun and it's personal. Don't let anyone tell you how or what to enjoy.

James Joyce

"It's clearly a budget. It's got a lot of numbers in it."

— George W. Bush

MATHEMATICS ▶

Types of Numbers

You know what a number is, right? Bet you didn't know there are lots of different types. Here are a few of the most common:

Integers are whole numbers (i.e., no decimal places) and can be positive and negative, including zero:
. . . -5, -4, -3, -2, -1, 0, 1, 2, 3, 4 . . .

Natural numbers (also called the counting numbers) are positive integers:
1, 2, 3, 4, 5, 6 . . .

Rational numbers are ones that can be written as a fraction or ratio where the numerator and denominator are integers: e.g., 3/4, 5, 2.75

Irrational numbers are those that can't be written as fractions because the decimal form goes on forever. Any square root that is not perfect is an irrational number. For example, the square root of 4 is ±2, which is perfect and there-fore rational, but the square root of 2 is ±1.41421356 . . . and is irrational. Pi is also irrational = 3.14159265. . . .

Square numbers are numbers created by multiplying another number by itself. For example, 25 is a square number because it is 5 x 5 (or -5 x -5).

Prime numbers are integers greater than 1, which have no divisors except themselves and 1. The first 10 prime numbers are:
2, 3, 5, 7, 11, 13, 17, 19, 23, and 29.

Real numbers are all the above numbers.

Prime Factor Decomposition

One of the most important principles in pure mathematics is that any integer can be expressed as the product of its prime factors. In other words, all integers can be broken down into a unique set of prime numbers multiplied together.

Now, as math concepts go, that's pretty big. Many great mathematicians have spent their whole lives exploring this one idea. Aren't you glad you're not a great mathematician?

For example 30 = 2 x 3 x 5, so 2, 3, and 5 are its prime factors. Breaking a number into its factors is called prime factor decomposition.

To find the prime factor decomposition of 45, divide it by the first available prime number, in this case 3.

45 ÷ 3 = 15

Because 15 is not a prime number, find its first prime divisor, in this case 3 again.

45 = 5 x 3 x 3

The prime factors of 45 are 5 and 3, and prime factor decomposition is 5 x 3 x 3.

Fractions, Ratios, and Percentages

Don't you just hate them? Relax. They're not so scary once you get to know them. A fraction is the quotient of two integers such as 1/4, 2/8, 22/9, or 3/5.

1/4 means 1 divided by 4.
2/8 means 2 divided by 8.
3/5 means 3 divided by 5.

With fractions, the same number may be expressed in an infinite number of ways. For example, 5/20, 3/12, and 155/620 are all = 1/4 (or 0.25).

A fraction like 5/20 can be reduced by dividing the bottom number (denominator) by the top number (numerator) so that it can be written as 1/4. Fractions like 15/42 can be reduced by dividing both numbers by common factors. A common factor of 15 and 42 is 3, so the fraction can be written as 5/14, which cannot be reduced further.

Adding and Subtracting Fractions

Adding or subtracting two or more fractions is easy if the denominator is the same. All you do is add or subtract the top numbers and leave the denominator the same.

$$\frac{6}{5} + \frac{3}{5} + \frac{2}{5} = \frac{11}{5}$$

$$\frac{6}{5} - \frac{3}{5} - \frac{2}{5} = \frac{1}{5}$$

If the denominators are different, you must create a common denominator by multiplying the denominators together and then adding or subtracting the product of the two diagonals.

$$\frac{3}{5} + \frac{1}{3}$$

$$= \frac{3}{5} \times \frac{1}{3}$$

$$= \frac{(3 \times 3) + (5 \times 1)}{5 \times 3}$$

$$= \frac{14}{15}$$

$$\frac{3}{5} - \frac{1}{3}$$

$$= \frac{3}{5} \times \frac{1}{3}$$

$$= \frac{(3 \times 3) - (5 \times 1)}{5 \times 3}$$

$$= \frac{4}{15}$$

Multiplying Fractions

This is even easier. Multiply the two numerators and the two denominators.

$$\frac{3}{5} \times \frac{1}{3} = \frac{3}{15} = \frac{1}{5}$$

Dividing Fractions

Turn the second fraction upside down and multiply them together.

$$\frac{3}{5} \div \frac{1}{3} = \frac{3}{5} \times \frac{3}{1} = \frac{9}{5}$$

Ratios

The ratio is the relationship between two quantities. For example, if you have 4 apples and your friend has 12, this can be expressed as the ratio 4:12 or 1:3 (when cancelled down like a fraction).

If you have 60 apples that you want to share between yourself and a friend in the ratio 1:3, then you would divide 60 by the sum of the two numbers; for example, 60 divided by (1 + 3) = 60/4 = 15. Then multiply this result by the two numbers in the ratio to find each person's share; for example, 1 x 15 = 15 apples for you, and 3 x 15 = 45 apples for your friend.

Percentages

A percentage is a fraction whose denominator is 100.

For example 45% = 45/100
(which is 0.45 written in decimal).

To change a decimal into a percentage, multiply it by 100.
0.45 = 0.45 x 100 = 45%

To find A% of B, multiply A and B together and divide by 100.
So, 45% of 30 = $\frac{45 \times 30}{100}$ = $\frac{1350}{100}$ = 13.5

Sequences:
What Comes Next?

Remember doing this at school, looking for patterns in a sequence of numbers and try-ing to work out what should come next?

For example 1, 2, 3, 4, 5, 6, 7, 8 . . . is probably the most obvious progression. What comes next? The number 9, of course (if that was too difficult for you, you might want to take five before reading on).

Here's another easy one: 2, 4, 6, 8, 10, 12, 14, 16, 18, 20, 22. . . . The next number is 24 because you produce the next number in the sequence by adding 2 to the previous one.

In order to find the next number in a sequence you need to discover the pattern or the "nth term." In the above example, the nth term is 2n. This means you can find any term in the sequence by replacing n with the term. For instance, the eighth term in the above sequence is 2 x 8 (replace n with 8) = 16.

And now for a harder sequence . . . Sorry, but unless you're Stephen Hawking there is no easy way to crack the pattern. It is largely a matter of trial and error, though with practice, it becomes easier to recognize patterns within sequences. Okay, ready? Can you find the next three numbers in this sequence?
5, 20, 45, 80, 125 . . .

When a sequence looks this hard, you can bet that there is some squaring involved (multiplying numbers by themselves, e.g., $2^2 = 2 \times 2 = 4$; $3^2 = 3 \times 3 = 9$).

So lets look at n and n^2 and compare n^2 to the sequence.

n	=	1	2	3	4	5
n^2	=	1	4	9	16	25
sequence	=	5	20	45	80	125

It looks like n^2 has been multiplied by 5 in each case, so the nth term for this sequence is n^2 x 5. We've cracked it. Now we can work out any number in the sequence.

The next three numbers are the sixth, seventh, and eighth terms, so let's replace n by 6, 7, and 8.

n	=	6	7	8
n^2	=	36	49	64
sequence (n^2 x 5)	=	180	245	320

Isn't it easy when you know how?

The Fibonacci Sequence

Fibonacci is an important sequence that is created by adding together the two previous terms: 1, 1, 2, 3, 5, 8, 13, 21, 34, 55, 89, 144, 233, 377, 610, 987 . . .

It looks so simple, but don't even bother trying to work out the nth term. It's very complicated.

This sequence appears over and over again in mathematics, science, and nature. Count the petals or the way the leaves are grouped in any plant and you will find them set out in pairs, threes, fives, eights, or thirteens, and so forth. For example, sunflowers have rows of petals in pairs of 21, 34, 55, and 89. The seeds in its yellow head are set out in a number of spirals, usually 34 going one way, and 55 going another. Bees' honeycombs, seashells, and pinecones are prime examples of the complex simplicity of the beautiful Fibonacci sequence.

Who said math was boring?

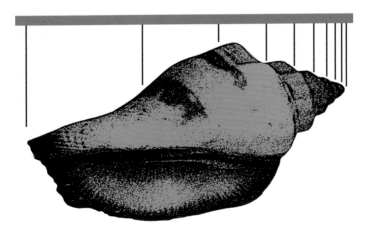

The Beauty of Prime Numbers

"To those who do not know mathematics it is difficult to get across a real feeling as to the beauty, the deepest beauty, of nature. . . . If you want to learn about nature, to appreciate nature, it is necessary to understand the language that she speaks in."
— Richard Feynman

A prime number is an integer greater than 1 that has no divisors except itself and 1. For example, 10 is not a prime number because its divisors are 2 and 5; 26 is not a prime number because its divisors are 2 and 13, but 11 is a prime number because its divisors are only itself and 1.

Prime numbers have fascinated mathematicians from the time of antiquity. More than 2,000 years ago, Euclid proved that there were infinitely many primes. This means that no matter how high you count, you will always find more prime numbers, although they become less and less frequent. In 1801 Carl Friedrich Gauss (one of the greatest mathematicians ever) wrote "the problem of distinguishing prime numbers from composite numbers and of resolving the latter into their prime factors is known to be one of the most important and useful in arithmetic."

Prime numbers aren't just for obsessive math students. They have practical uses, too. They form the basis of the advanced encryption technology that helps to keep online transactions safe. It is called the RSA algorithm, and it is secure because the absence of divisors means that even the most sophisticated computers cannot crack the code by looking for patterns. In fact, the world's biggest employer of mathematicians is America's National Security Agency, which is responsible for protecting United States communications and deciphering foreign communications.

Briefly, the RSA algorithm takes two large prime numbers and multiplies them together. This product, N, along with another number, E, comprises the public key. Then, a "one-way" function based on N and E is used to encrypt the message. Additionally, another value, D, which is based on the original two prime numbers, and N comprise the private key, and another one-way function is used to decrypt the message.

So, the task of factoring such a composite number becomes important if you're trying to break the encryption. So far, no methods have arisen that can factor such a number in a reasonable period of time. Hence, this algorithm is considered secure.

A Greek mathematician, around 240 B.C., came up with a clever way for finding all the small primes up to a given number (n), which is now called the Sieve of Eratosthenes. By making a list of all the integers less than or equal to n (greater than one) and striking out the multiples of all primes less than or equal to the square root of n, the numbers that are left will all be prime. For example, if you want to find all the primes between 1 and 100, first list all the odd numbers from 3 to 100 (don't bother with the even numbers—the only even prime is 2). The first prime number is 3, so cross out all of its multiples (i.e., 9, 15, 21, etc.). The next highest number left will be 5 (the second odd prime), so cross out all of its multiples (25, 35, 55, etc.). Repeat until

the next highest number left is greater than the square root of 100 (n); then you know that all the numbers remaining are prime.

This is such an effective method that a computer can work out primes faster than it can read a stored list of primes from its hard disk.

Finding small primes is easy. The real challenge is to discover bigger and bigger ones. In 1984 Samuel Yates coined the term "titanic prime" for any prime with at least 1,000 digits. Back then there were only 110 known titanic primes. Now with the advent of super computers there are more than 100,000 titanics, and the world's first billion-digit prime is just a few years away from being discovered.

Algebra:
Simultaneous Equations

A man walks into a bar and buys three beers and two bags of chips for $12. His friend arrives later and buys one beer and four bags of chips for $9. How much does a beer cost and how much for a bag of chips?

Believe it or not, hiding in the last paragraph are two simultaneous equations. Let's call a beer "b" and a bag of chips "c":

$$3b + 2c = 1200$$
$$1b + 4c = 900$$

There are two ways of solving these equations.

(1) You can multiply the first equation by, in this case, 2 to get: $6b + 4c = 2400$. Then, place the second equation underneath it—$1b + 4c = 900$—and take one from the other.

$$6b + 4c = 2400$$
$$1b + 4c = 900$$
$$5b = 1500$$
$$b = 300$$

Then substitute 300 for b in one of the equations to find c.

$$3(300) + 2c = 1200$$
$$900 + 2c = 1200$$
$$2c = 1200 - 900$$
$$2c = 300$$
$$c = 150$$

So a beer costs $3 and a bag of chips $1.50.

(2) Rearrange one of the equations to express b in terms of c.

$$1b + 4c = 900$$
$$b = 900 - 4c$$

Then, substitute it in the other equation.

$$3b + 2c = 1200$$
$$3(900 - 4c) + 2c = 1200$$
$$2700 - 12c + 2c = 1200$$
$$2700 - 10c = 1200$$
$$- 10c = 1200 - 2700$$
$$- 10c = -1500$$
$$c = 150$$

Then substitute 150 for c in one of the original equations to find b.

Averages

There isn't one, but four kinds of averages: mean, mode, median, and range.

Mean:

The mean is what most people understand by the term "average." The mean of a group of numbers is worked out by adding all the numbers and then dividing by the number of numbers.

For example, the average of the seven numbers 5, 7, 9, 15, 21, 24, and 37 is (5 + 7 + 9 + 15 + 21 + 24 + 37)/7 = 16.857

That's very straightforward, but often we work not with specific values, but a band of values. Then you must take a midpoint between the upper and lower values of each band, multiply each midpoint by the frequency (in the example below, the number of people), then add up everything in the fx column and divide by the total number of people.

Hours spent daily watching TV in a month	Number of People (f)	Midpoint (x)	fx
0 - 30	10	15	150
31 - 60	11	45.5	500.5
61 - 90	16	75.5	1208
91 - 120	18	105.5	1899
121 - 150	14	135.5	1897
151 - 180	8	165.5	1324
181 - 210	4	195.5	782
211 - 240	1	225.5	225.5
	82		7986

Here the approximate mean is
7986/82 = 97.39

Mode:

In a group of numbers, the mode is the "measure of primary tendency," or put more simply, the number that occurs most often. For example, the mode of 7, 6, 34, 3, 2, 4, 17, 1, 2, 22, and 31 is 2, because it occurs the most frequently.

Median:

In a group of numbers, the median is the one in the middle after you have arranged all the numbers in ascending order.

So, to find the median of 7, 6, 34, 3, 2, 4, 17, 1, 2, 22, and 31, we must first arrange them like this:

1, 2, 2, 3, 4, 6, 7, 17, 22, 31, 34

Now we can see that 6 is the median because it is in the middle.

Range:

This is found by subtracting the smallest value in the group from the largest. We've already put the above group of numbers in ascending order, so we can easily see that the range is 34 - 1 = 33.

Flow Charts

A flow chart is a pictorial representation of an algorithm. So what's an algorithm? A step-by-step problem-solving procedure with a finite number of steps.

You can make a flow chart for anything, and not only is it an invaluable way of writing down instructions, it can also reveal the strong and weak points in any process or task.

A basic flow chart uses these three boxes joined with arrows.

- Each shape corresponds to a step or decision point in the process.

- The lines indicate to the user which path to take.

- The text describes each part of the procedure.

This is used for the start or
end of the procedure.

This is an instruction box.

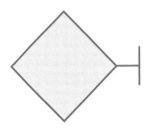

This is a decision box.

Here's a flow chart for making a cup of tea:

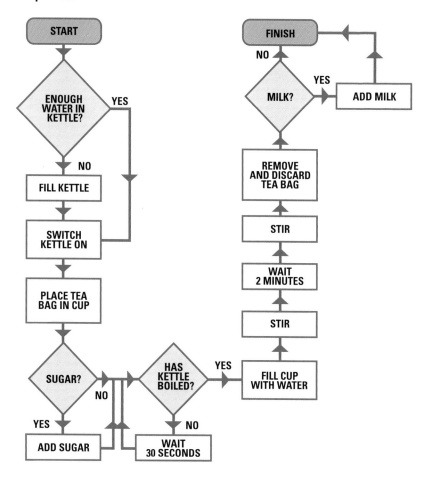

Geometry: Angles

We are surrounded by angles. Anywhere two lines cross or share the same endpoint, an angle is formed. Angles are measured in degrees. There are several types of angles, each with its own special name: acute, obtuse, reflex, right, complementary, supplementary, vertical, alternate interior, alternate exterior, and corresponding.

Acute Angle:
This measures between 0 and 90 degrees.

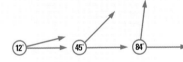

Obtuse Angle:
This measures between 90 and 180 degrees.

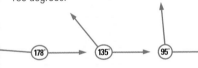

Reflex Angle:
This measures between 180 and 360 degrees.

Right Angle
This measures 90 degrees exactly. If two lines meet at a right angle they are perpendicular to each other.

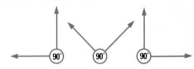

Complementary Angles
Two angles are complementary if they add up to 90 degrees. Each angle is the complement of the other.

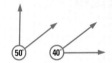

Supplementary Angles
Two angles are supplementary if they add up to 180 degrees. Each angle is the supplement of the other.

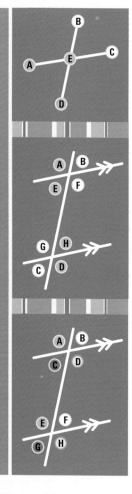

Vertically Opposite Angles

When two lines cross, the angles opposite each other are known as vertically opposite angles and have the same degree measurement. In this example the angles AEB and DEC are vertically opposite angles. So too are AED and BEC.

Alternate Angles

When two parallel lines (straight lines which do not intersect) are both intersected by a third line, angles A and D are alternate exterior angles and have the same degree measurement. B and C are also alternate exterior angles.

Angles E and H are alternate interior angles and have the same degree measurement. G and F are also alternate interior angles. Interior angles (e.g., G and H) always add up to 180 degrees.

Corresponding Angles

When two parallel lines are both intersected by a third line, angles A and E are corresponding angles and have the same degree measurement. B and F, C and G, and D and H are also corresponding angles.

Adjacent Angles

A and B are adjacent angles and add up to 180 degrees. So too are A and C, B and D, C and D, E and F, F and H, H and G, and G and E.

- *The angles around a point always add up to 360 degrees.*
- *The angles in a triangle always add up to 180 degrees.*
- *The angles in a quadrilateral (a four-sided shape) always add up to 360 degrees.*

Probability

Probability is the chance that something will happen. It is always somewhere between 0 (impossible) and 1 (certain).

If you flip a coin nine times and get nine heads in a row, is the tenth throw more likely to produce a head or tail?

Those who don't understand the principles of probability might be tempted to say, "the next one must be a tail," but, of course, the probability is always the same for each throw (assuming no trickery or cheating is involved). The probability of throwing a head is 1/2 (or 1 in 2) and the probability of throwing a tail is also 1/2 (1 in 2) because there are two equally likely outcomes to the flip of a coin.

However, it is easy to see why people get confused, because the probability of throwing ten heads in a row is very small (1 in 1024). Why? Because the probability of a sequence of events is the result of multiplying the probabilities of each event together.

The probability of throwing one head is 1/2. The probability of throwing two heads is 1/2 x 1/2 = 1/4. The probability of throwing three heads is 1/2 x 1/2 x 1/2 = 1/8 . . . and so on. The probability of throwing ten heads is 1/2 x 1/2 x 1/2 x 1/2 x 1/2 x 1/2 x 1/2 x 1/2 x 1/2 x 1/2 = 1/1024.

When you throw a die, the chance of throwing a 3 is 1 in 6 or 1/6 because there are six equally likely outcomes to the throw of a die (1, 2, 3, 4, 5, 6). The sum of all possible outcomes must always add up to 1. When you throw two or more dice and add them together, the probability of getting a two (1 + 1) is 1/6 x 1/6 = 1/36 but the probability of getting a seven is 1/6 because there are six ways of doing it out of a possible 36 outcomes: (1 + 6), (2 + 5), (3 + 4), (4 + 3), (5 + 2), and (6 + 1).

SCORE	PERMUTATIONS	PROBABILITY
2	(1+1)	1/36
3	(1+2) (2+1)	2/36 = 1/18
4	(1+3) (2+2) (3+1)	3/36 = 1/12
5	(1+4) (2+3) (3+2) (4+1)	4/36 = 1/9
6	(1+5) (2+4) (3+3) (4+2) (5+1)	5/36
7	(1+6) (2+5) (3+4) (4+3) (5+2) (6+1)	6/36 = 1/6
8	(2+6) (3+5) (4+4) (5+3) (6+2)	5/36
9	(3+6) (4+5) (5+4) (6+3)	4/36 = 1/9
10	(4+6) (5+5) (6+4)	3/36 = 1/12
11	(5+6) (6+5)	2/36 = 1/18
12	(6+6)	1/36

Notice that the total number of permutations (possible outcomes) is 36 and the sum of the probabilities is 1.

Each permutation has a 1/36 chance of occurring, so to find out the chance of throwing a 7 we add the probabilities together:

1/36 + 1/36 + 1/36 + 1/36 + 1/36 + 1/36 = 6/36 = 1/6.

Likewise, the chance of throwing a 4 is 1/36 + 1/36 + 1/36 = 3/36 = 1/12.

Math is Fun

If you think math isn't fun, you're wrong. No, really. Haven't the last few pages been a blast?

Here are four puzzles that are baffling and intriguing, sometimes for very complicated mathematical reasons. They are included here to show that you don't always have to understand math to enjoy it!

Four-Color Jigsaw

If you think math got kind of complicated once you got past the coloring-in stage, here's a puzzle you'll enjoy. It is impossible to color in this picture with less than four colors, such that each piece of the jigsaw is colored in and no adjacent pieces share the same color. Try it. This is true of any jigsaw, regardless of size and number of pieces.

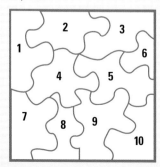

Möbius Strip

Stick the two ends of a strip of paper together with a half twist to make a Möbius strip. Now cut it down the middle as shown and you will get one larger loop. Cut it again and you will get two interlocking loops.

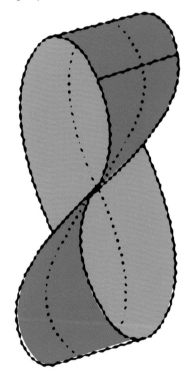

Reach the Moon

How many times do you have to fold a piece of paper to reach the moon?

The answer is 46! Say a piece of paper is 0.0004 inches thick—after one fold in half, it will be 0.0008 inches thick; after 2, it's 0.0016 inches, then 0.0032 inches, until after 46 it would be 28,147,497,671.0656 inches thick, which is 444,247 miles. The average distance to the moon is 237,675 miles, so it would almost reach to the moon and back.

Zeno's Paradox

If you want to walk from A to B, first you must cross half the distance (you're halfway there), then you must cover half the remaining distance (you're 3/4 of the way there) then you must cross half the remaining distance (you're 7/8 of the way there) and so on. You will never reach your destination because you will always have a fraction left to cross. Therefore, all motion is impossible! Or is it?

"If it weren't for electricity we'd all be watching television by candlelight."

— George Gobol

SCIENCE ▶

Atoms

The Ancient Greeks believed the four elements—earth, air, fire, and water—to be the fundamental constituents of the universe. Most of us would agree that they were way off. In fact, the universe is built out of 92 natural elements, and there are a further 24 elements that have been created by scientists (but they are very unstable, so only last for a fraction of a second before turning into one of the original 92 elements).

An element is a substance that can't be divided into anything more simple by normal chemical means. Some are metals, non-metals, solids, liquids, or gases. But what makes them elements is that they are composed of one type of atom. For example, hydrogen is made up of hydrogen atoms and nothing else; gold is made of gold atoms and nothing else.

An atom is made up of three major components—protons, neutrons, and electrons.

The center of an atom is called the nucleus, made up of a mixture of positively charged protons and neutrally charged neutrons. Negatively charged electrons orbit around the nucleus. Usually there are equal numbers of protons and electrons, which makes atoms electrically neutral.

What makes atoms different from each other is their number of protons. This is called the atomic number. Nitrogen has seven protons in each atom, so its atomic number is seven.

Atoms of the same element will always have the same number of protons (otherwise they would be different elements), but they may have different numbers of neutrons, making them isotopes, or different versions of the same element. For example, the most common isotope of helium has two neutrons, but helium 3 is an isotope with 3 neutrons. (It could be the perfect fuel source for the twenty-first century in nuclear fusion, except that there's hardly any on earth. But there are thought to be about a million tons on the moon. Just two tons could supply the entire United States' energy needs for a month.)

The elements are arranged in a periodic table in the order of their atomic number in 18 columns (groups) and nine rows (periods).

When two or more atoms from different elements are held together by chemical bonds, they form a molecule. For example, a molecule of water consists of two atoms of hydrogen and one of oxygen (which is why it is called H_2O). Water is a therefore known as a compound (of elements).

1 H																	2 He
3 Li	4 Be											5 B	6 C	7 N	8 O	9 F	10 Ne
11 Na	12 Mg											13 Al	14 Si	15 P	16 S	17 Cl	18 Ar
19 K	20 Ca	21 Sc	22 Ti	23 V	24 Cr	25 Mn	26 Fe	27 Co	28 Ni	29 Cu	30 Zn	31 Ga	32 Ge	33 As	34 Se	35 Br	36 Kr
37 Rb	38 Sr	39 Y	40 Zr	41 Nb	42 Mo	43 Tc	44 Ru	45 Rh	46 Pd	47 Ag	48 Cd	49 In	50 Sn	51 Sb	52 Te	53 I	54 Xe
55 Cs	56 Ba	71 Lu	72 Hf	73 Ta	74 W	75 Re	76 Os	77 Ir	78 Pt	79 Au	80 Hg	81 Ti	82 Pb	83 Bi	84 Po	85 At	86 Rn
87 Fr	88 Ra	103 Lr	104 Rf	105 Db	106 Sg	107 Bh	108 Hs	109 Mt	110 Ds								

57 La	58 Ce	59 Pr	60 Nd	61 Pm	62 Sm	63 Eu	64 Gd	65 Tb	66 Dy	67 Ho	68 Er	69 Tm	70 Yb
89 Ac	90 Th	91 Pa	92 U	93 Np	94 Pu	95 Am	96 Cm	97 Bk	98 Cf	99 Es	100 Fm	101 Md	102 No

The Human Body

Skeleton:
Your skeleton is made of 206 bones, which provide strength and protection and are joined together by short fibrous cords called ligaments, which provide stability for the joints and hold the bones in place. The end of each bone is covered with cartilage, which acts like a shock absorber to cushion and protect. If this cartilage degenerates, arthritis develops.

Teeth:
Your teeth are the hardest part of your entire body. They are covered in a layer of enamel that stops them from wearing down and protects them from chemicals in food. Because we are omnivores (we eat both plants and animals), our teeth are adapted to both tear food (front teeth—incisors and canines) and chew (back teeth—molars). Children have 20 teeth; the second set usually contains 32 (including the four wisdom teeth, which don't always appear).

Digestion:
Your body begins to break down food as soon as it enters your mouth. Chewing combined with enzymes in your saliva starts the digestion process. Food then travels through the esophagus to the stomach, where a very strong acid partly digests the food to produce chyme which travels into your small intestine. Here proteins are converted into amino acids; carbohydrates are broken down into a simple sugar called glucose; fats are turned into tiny droplets in the small intestine by bile that is produced in the liver and stored and released by the gallbladder. Nutrients are absorbed through the intestinal wall. Onwards to the large intestine, where some of the water and minerals are removed and "friendly" bacteria help further digestion, then through the colon to the rectum from which solid waste is excreted.

Muscles:
Your skeleton is covered with about 660 muscles that account for about half your body weight. They are made of lots of fibers that convert energy (from digestion) into action by contracting and releasing. They come in pairs because each muscle can only pull in one direction. Without muscles your body could not move. Your heart is also a muscle, one that is highly specialized for endurance and consistency.

Blood:

The average adult body contains eight pints of blood. It is produced in your bones and is the fluid which transports oxygen, food, hormones, and warmth to and removes waste products from every cell in your body. There are four blood types: A, B, AB, and O, combined with two Rhesus factors (+ and -). Each drop contains millions of cells in a clear liquid called plasma. The red blood cells from which blood gets its color contain hemoglobin, which enables them to carry oxygen. The white blood cells attack germs or infection and are always on the lookout for disease. After an injury, irregularly shaped, colorless platelets gather at the site of the wound and then break down to form a threadlike structure called fibrin to trap blood cells and form a clot.

Circulation:

Your blood is pumped at very high pressure through about 100,000 miles of blood vessels by your heart, which beats about 100,000 times each day. With each beat, the top of the heart (atrium) contracts, forcing blood from the lungs into the lower part (ventricle), which contracts a fraction of a second later, sending blood away from the heart in the arteries. The veins bring the deoxygenated (a bluish color) blood back to the heart where it is pumped into the lungs.

Skin:

The whole body is covered with this tough, flexible layer that forms a protective barrier and helps to regulate body temperature. It is made of two main layers. The outer epidermis consists of about 25 smaller layers of dead skin and a single layer of dividing cells. The lower dermis is much thicker and elastic, giving skin its stretchiness. It also contains hair follicles, sweat glands, nerve endings, and capillaries (tiny blood vessels).

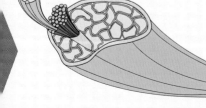

Eighteen Physical Laws

Newton's Three Laws of Motion:
1. Every object persists in its state of rest or uniform motion in a straight line unless it is compelled to change that state by forces impressed upon it.

2. The relationship between an object's mass, m, its acceleration, a, and the applied force, F, is F = ma.

3. For every action there is an equal and opposite reaction.

Boyle's Law:
For a fixed amount of gas at a fixed temperature, the pressure and the volume are inversely proportional.

Newton's Law of Cooling:
The rate of heat loss of a body is proportional to the difference in temperatures between the body and its surroundings.

Kepler's Laws of Planetary Motion:
1. The orbit of a planet around a star is an ellipse with the star at one focus.

2. A line joining a planet and its star sweeps out equal areas during equal intervals of time.

3. The square of the sidereal period of an orbiting planet (the time that it takes the object to make one full orbit around the sun, relative to the stars) is directly proportional to the cube of the orbit's semimajor axis (one half the major axis, running from the center, through a focus, and to the edge of the ellipse).

Archimedes' Principle:
When a body is submerged in a fluid it will be buoyed up by a force equal to the weight of the displaced fluid.

Law of Conservation of Energy:
In a closed system, the amount of energy is constant, irrespective of its changes in form; energy can neither be created nor destroyed.

Heisenberg's Uncertainty Principle:

In quantum mechanics, two complementary parameters (such as position and momentum) cannot both be measured accurately; the more closely you measure one, the less you can measure the other.

Joule's First Law:

The heat Q produced when a current L flows through a resistance R for a specified time t is given by $Q = L^2Rt$.

Joule's Second Law:

The internal energy of an ideal gas is independent of its volume and pressure, depending only on its temperature.

First Law of Thermodynamics:

The change in internal energy of a system is the sum of the heat transferred to or from the system and the work done on or by the system.

Second Law of Thermodynamics:

The entropy—a measure of the unavailability of a system's energy to do useful work—of a closed system tends to increase with time.

Third Law of Thermodynamics:

For changes involving only perfect crystalline solids at absolute zero, the change of the total entropy is zero.

Zeroth Law of Thermodynamics:

If two bodies are each in thermal equilibrium with a third body, then all three bodies are in thermal equilibrium with each other.

Newton's Law of Universal Gravitation:

Two bodies attract each other with equal and opposite forces; the magnitude of this force is proportional to the product of the two masses and is also proportional to the inverse square of the distance between the centers of mass of the two bodies.

Sixty Inventions and Discoveries

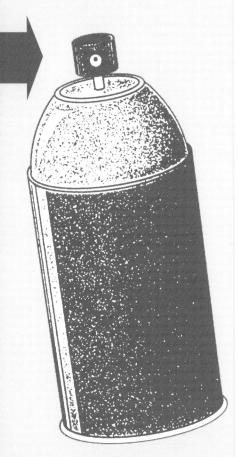

1. **Aerosol can** *(pressurized)*: Lyle D. Goodhue, U.S., 1941

2. **Air conditioning**: Willis Carrier, U.S., 1902

3. **Anesthetic** *(ether)*: Crawford W. Long, U.S., 1842

4. **Antibiotics** *(first use of bacteria to treat disease)*: Louis Pasteur, France, 1887

5. **Aspirin**: Felix Hoffman, Germany, 1899

6. **Atom** *(nuclear theory)*: Ernest Rutherford, England, 1911

7. **Automobile**: Karl Benz, Germany, 1885

8. **Autopilot** *(for aircraft)*: Elmer A. Sperry, U.S., 1909

9. **Bakelite**: Leo H. Baekeland, U.S., 1909

10. **Ballpoint pen**: Laszlo Biró, Hungary, 1938

11. **Bicycle**: Karl von Drais de Sauerbrun, Germany, 1817

12. **Braille**: Louis Braille, France, 1829

13. **Cement**: Joseph Aspdin, England, 1824

14. **Coca-Cola**: John Pemberton, U.S., 1886

15. **DNA** *(discovery of the double-helix)*: Francis H. Crick, England and James D. Watson, U.S., 1953

16. **Dynamite**: Alfred Nobel, Sweden, 1867

17. **Dynamo**: Michael Faraday, England, 1831

18. **Electric arc lamp**: Sir Humphry Davy, England, 1801

19. **Electric battery**: Alessandro Volta, Italy, 1800

20. **Frozen food** *(commercial freezing process)*: Clarence Birdseye, U.S., 1924

21. **Helicopter**: Heinrich Focke, Germany, 1936

22. **Hot-air balloon**: Joseph-Michel and Jacques-Étienne Montgolfier, France, 1783

23. **Insulin** *(first extracted)*: Frederick G. Banting, Charles H. Best, Canada, 1921

24. **Light bulb**: Thomas Edison, England, 1879

25. **Locomotive engine**: George Stephenson, England, 1812

26. **Loom** *(flying shuttle)*: John Kay, England, 1733

27. **Loom** *(mechanized)*: Edmund Cartwright, England, 1786

28. **Machine gun:** Richard J. Gatling, U.S., 1861

29. **Microwave oven:** Percy L. Spencer, U.S., 1947

30. **Parachute:** Sebastien Lenormand, France, 1783

31. **Penicillin:** Alexander Fleming, Scotland, 1928

32. **Photography** *(darkening of silver salts by light)*:
Johann H. Schulze, Germany, 1727

33. **Pianoforte:** Bartolomeo Cristofori, Italy, 1700

34. **Pistol** *(revolver)*: Samuel Colt, U.S., 1835

35. **Post-It note:** Art Fry, U.S., 1974

36. **Printing** *(modern Western)*: Johann Gutenberg,
Germany, 1450

37. **Prozac** *(fluoxetine)*: Bryan B. Malloy, Scotland, and
Klaus K. Schmiegel, U.S., 1972

38. **Radar:** Christian Hülsmeyer, Germany, 1904

39. **Radio:** Guglielmo Marconi, Italy, 1895

40. **Refrigerator:** Alexander Twining, U.S.,
James Harrison, Australia, 1850

41. **Rocket** *(liquid-fuel)*: Robert H. Goddard, U.S., 1926

42. **Rocket** *(solid-fuel)*: William Congreve, England, 1804

43. **Rubber** *(vulcanized)*: Charles Goodyear, U.S., 1839

44. **Safety matches:** J. E. Lundstrom, Sweden, 1855

45. **Safety pin:** Walter Hunt, U.S., 1849

46. **Sewing machine:** Barthélemy Thimonnier, France, 1830

47. **Spermatozoa:** Antoni van Leeuwenhoek,
The Netherlands, 1677

48. **Stethoscope:** René T. H. Laënnec, France, 1819

49. **Teflon** *(polytetrafluoroethene)*: DuPont Corp., U.S., 1943

50. **Telephone:** Alexander Graham Bell, U.S., 1876

51. **Telescope:** Hans Lippershey, The Netherlands, 1608

52. **Thermometer: (1) Water:** Galileo Galilei, Italy, 1593;
(2) Mercury: Daniel Gabriel Fahrenheit, Germany, 1714

53. **Transistor:** John Bardeen, Walter H. Brattain,
William B. Shockley, U.S., 1947

54. **Turbojet aircraft engine:** Frank Whittle, England, 1941

55. **Typewriter:** William Austin Burt, U.S., 1829

56. **Vaccination:** Edward Jenner, England, 1796

57. **Vacuum cleaner:** Ives W. McGaffey, U.S., 1869

58. **VCR: (1) Betamax:** Sony Corp., Japan, 1975;
(2) VHS: Matsushita Corp., Japan, 1975

59. **X-rays:** Wilhelm K. Roentgen, Germany, 1895

60. **Zip fastener:** Whitcomb L. Judson, U.S., 1893

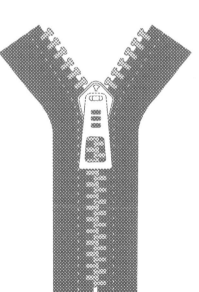

Evolution and Natural Selection

Many people today have a fuzzy under-standing of the theory of natural selec-tion. We are all familiar with the phrase "survival of the fittest," but this is a reductive and incomplete summary that risks misrepresenting the core mechanism. Others might summarize natural selection as, "It's like giraffes have grown long necks because they have to eat the leaves from tall trees." Again this is so vague as to be wrong (in fact, this very example was used by Larmarck in 1801 to show, incorrectly, that giraffes' necks have grown longer because of stretching to reach high leaves, a characteristic that was then passed on to their offspring).

Charles Darwin's theory of evolution is founded on the observation that the population of organisms should grow exponentially until it reaches infinity. That this is clearly not the case can be explained by the presence of limited resources. Therefore, there must be a "struggle," or competition, for these resources, which keeps the population in check. Parents who have certain traits that enable them to survive and reproduce will contribute disproportionately to the next generation, and since offspring tend to inherit traits from their parents, those offspring will themselves contribute disproportionately to the subsequent generation.

But Darwin didn't stop there. He showed that all creatures change over time and that the ones that are alive today are different from those that came before. Furthermore, he showed that if we look back far enough, all creatures are descended from a common ancestor, but have branched away from each other through adaptive radiation, first into varieties of the same species and ultimately into separate species.

He based this conclusion upon observation of 13 species of finches in the Galápagos Islands during his five-year journey as an unpaid naturalist aboard HMS *Beagle*, which set sail in 1831. He noticed that each species had evolved differently, most noticeably in beak shape, because the envi-ronment in each case was slightly different and each beak shape was associated with a different diet.

But Darwin did not suggest that the environment created the beak shape—he correctly believed that the variation already existed (since individuals within a given population are subtly different) and those birds were favored by their increased ability to find food and reproduce as a result of that variation. The birds with less useful beak shapes died out, not because they were ineffective, but because they weren't the most effective in the competition for limited resources.

When Darwin published his famous *On the Origin of Species by Means of Natural Selection* on November 24, 1859, it sold out immediately and caused a storm among religious and scientific communities. Many people believed then, as they do now, that the world was fixed in the state in which it had been created by God. But increasing fossil evidence and the efforts of geologist Charles Lyell showed that the world was much older than 6,000 years, convincing most educated people in the late nineteenth century that organisms change through time, and eventually to the previously unthinkable and blasphemous notion that humans are descended from apes.

Darwin's Finches

Freud, Jung, and the Unconscious

Sigmund Freud, known as the father of psychoanalysis, was one of the most influential thinkers of the twentieth century. Jung was one of his students, but broke away to form a rival school of psychology.

Freud was born in Frieberg, Moravia, in 1856, and concentrated initially on biology. After spending time in Paris where he was influenced by the French neurologist and hypnotism pioneer Jean Charcot, and colleague and friend Josef Breuer, who encouraged his hysterical patients to talk to him, Freud developed the theory that neuroses are caused by deeply repressed past traumas. He encouraged his patients to recall and confront these repressed experiences, then published his ideas in *Studies in Hysteria* in 1895.

At this point Freud parted company from Breuer, who felt that Freud placed too much emphasis on the sexual origins of neuroses. Five years later Freud published *The Interpretation of Dreams,* which showed how analyzing dreams was one way of unlocking secrets within the unconscious, but it was a further eight years before his ideas were recognized by the psychoanalytical community. His reputation and fame continued to grow, and he published more than 20 volumes of work before his death from cancer in 1939 (he was a very heavy cigar smoker).

Freud's own childhood greatly influenced his ideas about the mind. His father had two adult sons by an earlier marriage, one of whom Freud came to identify as a surrogate father figure. He fantasized about killing his own father and had sexual feelings for his mother. Thus was born the Oedipal complex (from the play by Sophocles in which Oedipus unknowingly kills his father and sleeps with his mother).

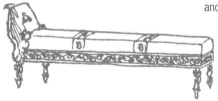

His theory of the unconscious was also influenced by contemporary physics, which was focusing on the idea that energy in a physical system cannot be created or destroyed (Helmholz's principle of the conservation of energy). Freud treated the human personality as an energy-system driven by "psychic energy." He also believed that for every neurosis (effect) there must be a repressed trauma (cause), and that we are governed by mental processes over which we have no control (and are unaware).

This energy system consisted of three parts. The first part he called the Id, which represents our most basic animal instincts (the sexual and aggressive—also described as Libido or Eros—life instinct, and the death instinct also known as Thanatos). The second part he called the Ego, which is logical and acts as a mediator between the Id's desires and external reality. It's a regulator without which we would be destroyed by acting out our naked desires, because the Id is nonverbal and pays no attention to what is possible (our fantasies and deepest desires are rarely attainable in the real world, and even when they are, they usually cause destruction and pain). The third is called the Superego, which is another word for conscience or morality acquired by parental and societal conditioning. Neuroses appear when pathogenic conflicts arise between these three parts. Freud has been criticized for placing so much emphasis on our desire for sexual gratification, but actually he said that we are driven to acquire and enhance bodily pleasure (a much wider concept that can encompass many obsessive and addictive behaviors, such as drug abuse and eating disorders, although you don't have to be a Freudian to see that there is a connection between these behaviors and sexuality).

Carl Jung was born in 1875 and did not accept Freud's contention that sexual gratification was the primary motivation behind behavior. His take on psychic energy was that, while he accepted the existence of a personal unconscious, he also believed that we inherit material from a collective unconscious passed down to us through evolution along with our physical characteristics. This, he argued, explains common themes, patterns, myths, and images that occur in different cultures. He called these commonalities "archetypes."

What is $E = MC^2$?

When Einstein studied the motion of a body, he had a startling insight about the body's mass and energy that he then went on to prove with mathematics—and he did all this in his spare time! By day he was a 26-year-old patent examiner.

Einstein created the Special Theory of Relativity, which states that the speed of light is constant, no matter what speed you are traveling at; and also, that all observers moving at constant speed should observe the same physical laws.

For example, if you were to throw a ball at 50 mph from the front of a train traveling at 100 mph, the ball would leave your hand at a speed of 150 mph. But if instead you shone a torch, the light would travel forward at the speed of light, not 100 mph faster.

In other words, space and time are relative (and famously, moving clocks appear to tick more slowly relative to stationary ones). Which leads to his famous insight that mass (or matter) and energy are equivalent, summed up in the famous equation: $E=MC^2$ which says that energy (E) is equal to mass (m) multiplied by the speed of light (c) squared.

This means that Newton was wrong (but not so that you'd notice in ordinary circumstances, only when traveling at speeds close to the speed of light), because his calculations depended upon space and time being absolute.

$E=MC^2$ means that mass is a form of energy and vice versa. Since the speed of light squared is an huge number (186,000 miles per second), a small amount of mass can be converted to an enormous quantity of energy. Or, if there's enough energy, some of it can be converted to mass. Nuclear reactors and atomic bombs work by splitting atoms with very small amounts of mass to release very large amounts of energy.

Later Einstein expanded his Special Theory into the General Theory of Relativity, which proposed that matter causes space to curve. Picture a watermelon on a large rubber sheet. The watermelon makes an indentation in the rubber sheet. If you dropped a grape onto the sheet it would roll towards the watermelon, not because both fruits are attracted by a mysterious force (which Newton called "gravity") but because it will roll into the hollow (or warped space) made by the heavier watermelon.

Quantum Theory

This is a theory developed in the first three decades of the twentieth century that explains the nature and behavior of matter and energy on the atomic and subatomic level. With Einstein's Theory of Relativity, it forms the basis for modern physics and even has practical applications in computing and cryptography.

In 1900 a physicist named Max Planck theorized that energy was absorbed or emitted from matter in discreet packets of energy that he called "quanta." This was a very controversial suggestion, since conventional thinking was that energy passed between matter in a continuous flow. Planck argued that we observe many millions of these quanta exchanges in rapid succession, which gives the illusion that it is a continual flow. This is rather like a person standing in front of an Impressionist painting refusing to believe that the image that he is viewing is, on closer inspection, composed of thousands of tiny dots of paint.

Planck's critics were many and vociferous, but in 1902 Albert Einstein designed an experiment demonstrating what later became known as the "Photoelectric Effect," which

proved Planck correct. In 1924, Louis de Broglie proposed that, on the atomic and subatomic levels, energy and matter may behave as either particles or waves (the principle of wave-particle duality). But the most intriguing feature of quantum physics is that, as Werner Heisenberg proposed in 1927, it is impossible to measure two complementary values simultaneously, such as the position and momentum of a subatomic particle, because the very act of measurement alters the result.

An intriguing conundrum known as Schrödinger's Cat demonstrates the uneasy relationship between the classical and quantum worlds. Devised by Austrian physicist Erwin Schrödinger in 1935, the theoretical experiment places a cat in a light-proof and sound-proof box. Inside the box is a vial of cyanide. A single electron is fired from a particle accelerator and an electron detector measures the "spin" of the particle, which can only be one of two possible values (+1/2 or -1/2). If the value is +1/2, a hammer is triggered, breaking the vial and the cat dies. If the value is -1/2, nothing happens. Once the particle has been fired the cat will either be dead or alive, and thus the "spin" of the particle has been measured, but the value cannot be known until the box is opened and the cat observed to be either dead or alive. Here lies the contradiction—the spin of the particle can only be measured by opening the box, and therefore it preserves its quantum state until this moment. But this means that the cat must be both dead and alive; it is in both states simultaneously as long as we don't look to check. This principle is called superposition (or the Copenhagen interpretation of quantum theory) and means that probabilities only become certainties through measurement and observation (rather like the familiar concept of trees falling in forests with nobody there to hear them).

The second interpretation of quantum theory is the many-worlds theory (favored by Stephen Hawking), which suggests that these probabilities are expressed in parallel universes.

This all may sound fanciful, nevertheless this "quantum uncertainty" leads to some very interesting applications, not least in computing and cryptography. Scientists are currently trying to engineer quantum computers that will outperform any of the binary computers that perform calculations one at a time, albeit extremely fast.

A quantum processor can exploit the uncertainty principle to perform a huge number of calculations simultaneously. Quantum cryptography exploits the way in which a quantum state is destroyed by measurement to make the act of breaking a code impossible, because it would alter the code and alert the users to the intrusion. Quantum codes are already being used for a dedicated line between the White House and Pentagon in Washington, links between key military sites, and major defense contractors.

A Brief History of the Big Bang

In the late 1920s the American astronomer Edwin Hubble, after whom the Hubble telescope is named, observed that distant stars and galaxies are moving away from Earth in every direction and that the farther away an object is, the faster it is traveling. This implies that the universe must have once been much smaller—so small, in fact, that it had zero size, infinite mass, and infinite heat.

The good news is that, since the Big Bang, the earth has been cooling down. One second afterward, the temperature of the universe dropped to about 10 thousand million degrees (about a thousand times the temperature at the center of the sun)—quite a big fall from infinity. About a minute and a half later, the temperature was a chilly one thousand million degrees (the temperature of the hottest stars).

From our point of view, not much happened then for about 10 billion years, when our solar system started forming from the leftovers of earlier stars rotating in a big flattened spinning disk 580,000 trillion miles in diameter, which today we call the Milky Way.

It was another five billion years later that eighteenth-century theologian William Paley suggested "proof by design" as a means of explaining the complexity of the universe.

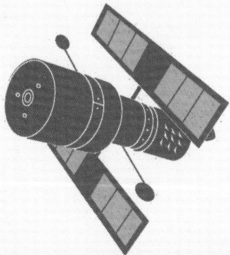

The Hubble Telescope

Birth of Computers

The first freely programmable computer was invented in 1936 by Konrad Zuse, a German engineer for the Henschel Aircraft Company in Berlin. It was called the Z1 and was a mechanical binary calculating machine that had a memory and could keep track of intermediate results for use later. Zuse used it to develop key technologies that now form the basis of modern computing, including floating-point arithmetic and the yes/no principle (base 2). He used old movie film to store his data, because paper was scarce. In 1946 he even wrote the first programming language called "Plankalkül" and used it to write the world's first chess-playing program. Unable to secure funding from the Nazi government, he escaped to Switzerland and smuggled his final model-in-progress, the Z4, with him on a horse-drawn cart to Zürich.

While the Z1 was mechanical, the first electronic-digital computer was developed between 1939 and 1942 at Iowa State College by Professor John Atanasoff and graduate engineering student Clifford Berry. It was later named the ABC for the Atanasoff-Berry Computer. It weighed 700 pounds, was the size of a gaming machine, and contained over a mile of wire. It could perform one operation every 15 seconds (modern computers are about 200 billion times faster). Amazingly, while Atanasoff was away working with the government on military and defense projects during the war, the computer was dismantled and destroyed by the physics faculty during a spring cleaning. Only a few parts of this important artifact remain.

The next breakthrough was the Mark series of computers, built for the United States Navy by Howard Aiken and Grace Hopper at Harvard University beginning in 1944. The Mark I filled a room—it was 55 feet long, 8 feet high, and weighed 5 tons. The ENIAC (Electrical Numerical Integrator and Calculator) was even bigger—it took up 1,800 square feet, weighed 30 tons, and cost $500,000. It required so much power to operate that when it was switched on, the city of Philadelphia experienced near blackouts. It was a thousand times faster than its contemporaries, but required weeks to program.

The invention of the transistor to replace vacuum tubes revolutionized computers and enabled them to begin shrinking. Then Jack Kilby and Robert Noyce came up with the idea of replacing the hundreds of miles of wiring by placing all the components on a "chip" made of semiconductor material (germanium or silicon).

Today's computers use microprocessors, which were invented way back in 1971 by Intel Corp., but the next breakthrough will arrive in the form of quantum computers, which for the first time will be able to perform millions of calculations simultaneously, rather than linearly as they do currently.

"History is more or less bunk."

— Henry Ford

HISTORY ▶

Archaeology: A Load of Old Bones?

The term archaeology is made up from the Greek archaios, which means "ancient," and logos, which means "discourse." This study emerged as a formal discipline in the nineteenth and early twentieth centuries.

Archaeology seeks to understand how past human culture functioned and how humans behaved (as distinct from paleontology, which is the study of fossils of long-extinct animals, such as dinosaurs). Archaeologists do this by examining what they call the archaeological record— the material remains of previous human settlements, including fossils (preserved bones), the ruins of buildings, food remains, and human artifacts, such as tools, pottery, and jewelry.

Archaeological digs in Africa have uncovered the origins of humanity and the fossil remains of humans up to 4.5 million years ago. But, archaeology also examines more recent history. One recent research project involves analyzing the garbage of modern humans in cities across the United States.

There are many different branches of archaeology. Prehistoric archaeology examines ancient cultures that had not developed writing, whether it was 5,000 years ago in parts of southwestern Asia or as recently as the nineteenth century A.D. in central Africa. Historical archaeology examines past cultures that did use writing. Geoarchaeology examines the ancient landscape and environment. Ethnoarchaeology is the study of living people in order to deduce how past cultures might have functioned; for example, present-day and ancient hunter-gatherers share common features. Underwater archaeology uses special methods and sophisticated diving techniques to study shipwrecks and other archaeological sites that lie beneath water. Experimental archaeology uses models and reconstruction of sites and artifacts and even the growing of ancient varieties of crops and animals to learn about the past. Archaeological studies have three aims:

chronology (the age of the excavated
material), reconstruction (creating models),
and explanation (scientific hypotheses).

Increasingly, archaeologists are using
less intrusive methods, such as radar
and imaging techniques known as remote
sensing (from airplanes or spacecraft),
which reduce the need for excavation. It's
not all about digging up bones anymore.

**Chronology
Reconstruction
Explanation**

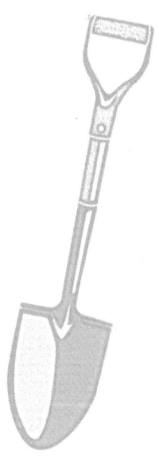

Twenty Battles

Agincourt:
Fought in Northern France on October 25, 1415 (St. Crispian's Day), as the heavily outnumbered army of King Henry V of England conquered that of Charles VI of France during the Hundred Years' War. Henry's speech to his army before the battle was made famous by Shakespeare in *Henry V*.

Battle of the Boyne:
On July 1, 1690, deposed King James II lost the English, Scottish, and Irish thrones to his son-in-law, William III, outside the town of Drogheda on the east coast of Ireland.

Bunker Hill:
On June 17, 1775, during the Siege of Boston in the American Revolutionary War, British forces, commanded by General Howe, drove Americans from their positions on Breed's Hill and Bunker Hill, but suffered major casualties with little overall benefit.

Cold Harbor:
Fought during the American Civil War from June 1 to June 3, 1864, near Cold Harbor, Virginia, it culminated in the slaughter of more than 13,000 Union soldiers at-tempting to advance to the Confederate entrenchment. The Confederates lost fewer than 2,000 men, and even they were shocked by the carnage caused by the folly of the Union commanders.

Dunkirk:
Between May 25 and June 3, 1940, during World War II, "Operation Dynamo" successfully rescued 338,226 Allied troops (aboard nearly 700 different vessels) who had become trapped against the coast on the Franco-Belgian border by the advancing German army.

Edgehill:
This first major, though inconclusive, conflict of the British Civil War took place on October 23, 1642, at Edgehill in Warwickshire between Charles I and Robert Devereux, Third Earl of Essex.

El Alamein:
This campaign was fought in the deserts of northern Egypt between July and November, 1942, and was a turning point in World War II. The Allied forces under the command of Bernard Montgomery ("Monty") breached the German lines and forced Erwin Rommel's retreat to Tunisia.

Gallipoli:

A poorly planned and badly executed Allied campaign to capture the Turkish peninsula of Gallipoli during 1915 in World War I. Intended to open up a sea lane to the Russians through the Black Sea, the attempt failed with more than 50 percent casualties on both sides.

Gettysburg:

A turning point of the American Civil War, Gettysburg was fought from July 1 to July 3, 1863, around the town of Gettysburg, Pennsylvania. General Robert E. Lee's 75,000-men army of Northern Virginia met General George G. Meade's 97,000-strong Union army of the Potomac. There were 51,000 casualties, and more men fought and died here than in any other battle on United States soil before or since.

Hastings:

This decisive Norman victory (William, Duke of Normandy) in the Norman Conquest of England (King Harold) on October 14, 1066, is the subject of the Bayeux Tapestry. It was the last time Britain was successfully invaded by a foreign power.

Iwo Jima:

The American and Japanese forces fought during February and March of 1945, the Pacific campaign of World War II. When the United States forces captured the island of Iwo Jima and its airfields, they suffered 25,000 casualties, with nearly 7,000 dead. In this single battle, the Marines earned over a quarter of the Medals of Honor awarded to Marines in World War II.

Little Bighorn:

In Montana from June 25 to June 26, 1876, five companies of the United States Cavalry, including one led by Colonel George A. Custer, were hugely outnumbered and subsequently wiped out by Sioux and Cheyenne Indians led by Chiefs Sitting Bull and Crazy Horse. It was one of the worst American military disasters in history.

The Battle of the Nile
(a.k.a. Battle of Aboukir Bay)

Fought on August 1 and 2, 1798, it was an important naval battle of the French Revolutionary War between victorious Admiral Horatio Nelson's British fleet and a French fleet under Vice-Admiral François-Paul Brueys d'Aigalliers.

Battle of Orléans:
Joan of Arc's first and greatest victory during the Hundred Years' War in 1429. She led the French army in freeing Orléans, which was under siege by the English.

The Battle of Québec:
A failed attempt on December 31, 1775, by American rebels, led by Benedict Arnold, to seize the Canadian city of Québec and secure Canadian assistance for the Revolutionary War.

Somme:
A five-month offensive between July and November 1916 in the Somme River area in France. It began with a massive week-long British artillery barrage that proved futile, since the Germans just sheltered in their dug-outs until the shelling stopped, then machine-gunned waves of British troops who were crossing no-man's land. On the first day alone the British lost 60,000 men. The battle ended in a stalemate, after torrential rain turned the trenches into a quagmire. There were more than 650,000 casualties on both sides, and although the British had relieved the French at Verdun, they had only advanced about five miles.

Stalingrad:
Fought during the winter of 1942, it was the first major Soviet victory of World War II and a turning point for the Allies. It claimed more lives than any other single conflict in the War but prevented the Nazis from capturing Russia and was a crucial factor in their eventual defeat.

Trafalgar:
The most important naval battle of the Napoleonic Wars. On October 21, 1805, the British Royal Navy led by Horatio Nelson destroyed a combined French and Spanish fleet, thereby ensuring British naval supremacy for the next 100 years.

Waterloo:
Fought on June 18, 1815, when the Duke of Wellington led the armies of the Grand Alliance and inflicted a final defeat on Emperor Napoleon Bonaparte.

Ypres:

Three battles of World War I (1914–1918) were fought in and around the town of Ypres, Belgium, a key part of an Allied battle line blocking a German advance to the English Channel. Both sides dug in after the First Battle (October to November 1914), beginning a long period of trench warfare. The Germans used poisonous chlorine gas during the Second Battle (April to May 1915), which ended after five weeks in a stalemate. The Third Battle (July to November 1917), also known as Passchendaele, took the total death toll for the three battles to more than 600,000.

United States Presidents

Every four years, American citizens elect their president on the first Tuesday after the first Monday in November. The president must be born in the United States and be at least 35 years old. No president may serve more than two terms. The candidates are decided by state primaries and caucuses. After the election the candidate with the most votes in each state wins all the electoral votes for that state. Each state's electoral votes is proportional to its population (which is why California, Florida, New York, and Texas are so important).

Past Presidents

1. George Washington (1789–1797)
2. John Adams (1797–1801)
3. Thomas Jefferson (1801–1809)
4. James Madison (1809–1817)
5. James Monroe (1817–1825)
6. John Quincy Adams (1825–1829)
7. Andrew Jackson (1829–1837)
8. Martin Van Buren (1837–1841)
9. William Henry Harrison (1841)
10. John Tyler (1841–1845)
11. James K. Polk (1845–1849)
12. Zachary Taylor (1849–1850)
13. Millard Fillmore (1850–1853)
14. Franklin Pierce (1853–1857)
15. James Buchanan (1857–1861)

A candidate needs 270 electoral votes to become president.

HISTORY

United States
Presidents

16. Abraham Lincoln (1861–1865)

17. Andrew Johnson (1865–1869)

18. Ulysses S. Grant (1869–1877)

19. Rutherford B. Hayes (1877–1881)

20. James A. Garfield (1881)

21. Chester A. Arthur (1881–1885)

22. Grover Cleveland (1885–1889)

23. Benjamin Harrison (1889–1893)

24. Grover Cleveland (1893–1897)

25. William McKinley (1897–1901)

26. Theodore Roosevelt (1901–1909)

27. William H. Taft (1909–1913)

28. Woodrow Wilson (1913–1921)

29. Warren G. Harding (1921–1923)

30. Calvin Coolidge (1923–1929)

31. Herbert Hoover (1929–1933)

32. Franklin D. Roosevelt (1933–1945)

33. Harry S. Truman (1945–1953)

34. Dwight D. Eisenhower (1953–1961)

35. John F. Kennedy (1961–1963)

36. Lyndon B. Johnson (1963–1969)

37. Richard M. Nixon (1969–1974)

38. Gerald R. Ford (1974–1977)

39. Jimmy Carter (1977–1981)

40. Ronald Reagan (1981–1989)

41. George H. W. Bush (1989–1993)

42. William J. Clinton (1993–2001)

43. George W. Bush (2001–present)

Eight died in office: William Henry Harrison, Zachary Taylor, Abraham Lincoln, James A. Garfield, William McKinley, Warren G. Harding, Franklin D. Roosevelt, and John F. Kennedy.

Seven were born in Ohio: Ulysses Grant, Rutherford Hayes, James Garfield, Benjamin Harrison, William McKinley, William Taft, and Warren Harding

Six owned slaves:
George Washington, Thomas Jefferson, James Madison, Andrew Jackson, James Polk, and Zachary Taylor

Four have been assassinated: Abraham Lincoln (by John Wilkes Booth), James Garfield (by Charles J. Guiteau), William McKinley (by Leon F. Czolgosz), and John F. Kennedy (by Lee Harvey Oswald)

Five have survived assassination attempts:
Andrew Jackson, Franklin D. Roosevelt, Harry Truman, Gerald Ford (twice), and Ronald Reagan

Four appear on Mount Rushmore:
George Washington, Thomas Jefferson, Theodore Roosevelt, and Abraham Lincoln

Three died on the Fourth of July: John Adams, Thomas Jefferson, and James Monroe

Three lost the popular vote but won the electoral college vote: Rutherford Hayes, Benjamin Harrison, and George W. Bush

Two ran unopposed: George Washington (both terms) and James Monroe (second term)

One won neither the popular vote nor the electoral college vote, and still became president: John Quincy Adams

One was elected to four terms: Franklin D. Roosevelt

One was a Roman Catholic: John F. Kennedy

One resigned: Richard Nixon

One never married: James Buchanan

Know Your Dinosaurs

Dinosaurs dominated the earth for more than 140 million years (that's 70 times longer than humans), until they vanished at the boundary between the Cretaceous and Tertiary periods, known as the K-T boundary. One of the most popular explanations is an asteroid impact that caused a dust cloud for 5,000 years, blocking out the sun's heat and light. Here are some of the major types of dinosaurs:

Ankylosaurus *("fused lizard")*:
A huge armored dinosaur, 25 to 35 feet long, covered with thick bony plates and possessing a club-like tail. Herbivore. Lived late Cretaceous period, 70 to 65 million years ago.

Apatosaurus *("deceptive lizard")*:
One of the largest land animals ever, 70 to 90 feet long and 15 feet tall, weighing 30 tons. Lifespan of more than 100 years. Herbivore. Lived late Jurassic period 157 to 146 million years ago.

Baryonyx *("heavy claw")*:
Named after its huge one-foot-long claws on its hands, 20 feet long, weighing more than two tons. Carnivore. Lived early Cretaceous period, about 125 million years ago.

Brachiosaurus *("arm lizard")*:
One of the tallest and largest dinosaurs, up to 50 feet tall and 100 feet long, weighing up to 60 tons. Herbivore. Lived middle to late Jurassic period, about 156 to 145 million years ago.

Compsognathus *("pretty jaw")*:
A bird-like dinosaur, the size of a chicken, weighing about eight pounds. Carnivore. Lived late Jurassic period, about 155 to 145 million years ago.

Deinonychus *("terrible claw")*:
Relatively light and agile with a large claw on its back feet. Up to 10 feet long and five feet tall, weighing up to 175 pounds. Carnivore. Lived during the Cretaceous Period, about 110 to 100 million years ago.

Diplodocus *("double beam")*:
One of the longest land animals,
90 feet long with a 26-foot-long neck and
a 45-foot-long whip-like tail. Weighing up
to 27 tons. Herbivore. Lived late Jurassic
period, from 155 to 145 million years ago.

Gallimimus *("chicken mimic")*:
A fast-running, ostrich-like dinosaur, up
to 20 feet long and was 11 feet tall, weighing about 260 pounds. Carnivore. Lived
late Cretaceous period 75 to 70 million
years ago.

Iguanodon *("Iguana tooth")*:
Plant-eater with teeth resembling a modern
iguana's and a bony spike on its fore legs,
30 feet long, 16 feet tall, weighing up to
five tons. Herbivore. Lived early Cretaceous
period, about 135 to 125 million years ago.

Kentrosaurus *("spiked lizard")*:
Small-brained dinosaur with long spikes
down its back, 17 feet long and weighing about two tons. Herbivore. Lived late
Jurassic period, about 156 to 150 million
years ago.

Maiasaurus *("mother lizard")*:
Duck-billed dinosaur which built nests and
nurtured its young. About 30 feet long,
eight feet tall, weighing up to two tons.
Herbivore. Lived late Cretaceous period
about 80 to 65 million years ago.

Mamenchisaurus *("Mamenchi [China] lizard")*:
Long-necked and long-tailed, up to 69 feet
long, weighing about 30 tons. Herbivore.
Lived late Jurassic period, about 156 to
145 million years ago.

Megalosaurus *("giant lizard")*:
The first dinosaur fossil ever discovered (in
1676), this giant walked on two legs. It was
up to 30 feet long, 10 feet tall, weighing
about one ton. Carnivore. Lived Jurassic
period, about 181 to 170 million years ago.

Mussaurus *("mouse lizard")*:
Only fossils of babies 16 inches long
have been found, but predicted adult
size is 26 feet long, weighing two tons.
Herbivore. Lived late Triassic about
215 million years ago.

Pachycephalosaurus *("thick-head lizard")*: Helmet-headed dinosaur with very thick skull surrounded by pebble-like bones. Up to 15 feet long and weighing two tons. Herbivore. Lived late Cretaceous period, about 76 to 65 million years ago.

Parasaurolophus *("like crested lizard")*: Duckbilled with a five-foot-long bony crest at the back of its head. Relatively fast. About 40 feet long and 15 feet tall, weighing three to four tons. Herbivore. Lived late Cretaceous period, about 76 to 65 million years ago.

TYRANNOSAURUS REX
("TYRANT LIZARD KING")

40 FT LONG
20 FT TALL
7 TONS

85-65 MILLION YRS.

Plateosaurus *("flat lizard")*:
One of the first tall, long-necked plant
eaters. About 26 feet long, weighing
about two tons. Herbivore. Lived late Triassic period, 222 to 219 million years ago.

Polacanthus *("many spines")*:
Squat dinosaur with a thick bony armor
of plates and spines. About 13 feet long
and five feet tall, weighing up to a ton.
Herbivore. Lived early Cretaceous period,
132 to 112 million years ago.

Protoceratops *("first horned face")*:
An ancestor of the Triceratops with
parrot-like beak and a large bony frill on
its head. Up to six feet long and three feet
tall, weighing about 900 pounds. Herbivore. Lived late Cretaceous period about
86 to 71 million years ago.

Seismosaurus *("earthquake lizard")*:
Long-necked and whip-tailed, up to 170
feet long and 84 feet tall, weighing about
100 tons. Herbivore. Lived late Jurassic
period, from 156 to 145 million years ago.

Stegosaurus *("roof lizard")*:
Has two rows of large bony plates running
along its back with four long spikes on its
tail. Up to 65 feet long, 14 feet tall, and

weighing three tons. Herbivore. Lived
late Jurassic period, about 156 to 140
million years ago.

Supersaurus *("super lizard")*:
Very large, long-necked, whip-tailed, 120
feet long and 65 feet tall, with a 40-foot-
long neck. Herbivore. Lived late Jurassic
period from 155 to 145 million years ago.

Triceratops *("three horned face")*:
Rhinoceros-like dinosaur with three horns
and a large bony frill on its head. Up to
30 feet long, 10 feet tall, weighing up to
seven tons. Herbivore. Lived Cretaceous
period about 72 to 65 million years ago.

Tyrannosaurus rex *("tyrant lizard king")*:
Huge and fierce predator. Up to 50 feet
long and 20 feet tall, weighing up to eight
tons. Carnivore. Lived late Cretaceous
period about 85 to 65 million years ago.

Velociraptor *("fast thief")*:
Fast-running, bipedal dinosaur with a
sickle-like claw on each foot. About six
feet long, three feet tall, weighing up
to 200 pounds. Carnivore. Lived late
Cretaceous period, about 85 to 80
million years ago.

Egyptian Mummification

Egypt was the first major African civilization. It began 6,000 years ago along the banks of the Nile River. Much of our understanding of Egyptians' culture has been provided by their belief in an afterlife and the great lengths to which they went in order to attain it.

They believed that an intact physical body was essential for the afterlife. The earliest Egyptians buried their dead in the baking sand, which quickly dried and preserved the bodies in a natural mummification process. Later they used coffins, and then embalming, to replace the activity of the sand.

The process was very expensive, time consuming, and very complicated, so it was only available to pharaohs and the very wealthy. It took more than two months to complete. First the body was washed with spices and a solution of natron (a natural salt mixture found along the Nile). Egyptians recognized that cleanliness was paramount to the preservation process, although they knew nothing of the action of bacteria in decomposition.

The second important step was to remove all moisture from the body. After the brain had been scooped out in a mushy mess through the nose and thrown away, all the internal organs were removed and sealed in four Canopic Jars (The Qebensnuet, Puamutef, Hapy, and Imsety), except for the heart, which was believed to be the seat of thought.

Body cavities were washed out with palm wine and myrrh and filled with bags of natron. Then the body was packed in a 600-pound pile of natron for 35 days at a temperature of 115 degrees Fahrenheit, during which it would lose nearly half its weight as water leeched out. Then the bags of natron were replaced by palm wine, spices, and wood shavings. After a mixture of five different oils had been rubbed into the skin—frankincense, myrrh, lotus, palm, and cedar—the body was ready for wrapping.

The origin of the word mummification comes from the bitumen like substance called "moumia" that was used to attach the linen strips during this stage. Each linen strip bore hieroglyphic inscriptions, and a total of six layers, and more than 20 pounds of linen were used.

Many intricate rituals were then performed. One of the most important of these was called the "The Opening of the Mouth" to rejuvenate all the senses.

The whole process took 70 days because the star Sirius disappears from the sky and returns 70 days later to signal the Egyptian New Year. The Egyptians equated this with the period between death and rebirth in the afterlife.

"Without geography, you're nowhere."

— Jimmy Buffett

GEOGRAPHY ▶

Gondwanaland and Continental Drift

In 1912 German meteorologist Alfred Wegener noticed that the bulge of eastern South America appeared to fit like a jigsaw piece into the western coast of Africa (Sir Francis Bacon noticed this, too, in the seventeenth century). Wegener came up with a hypothesis in which the world's continents were once joined into a single landmass. He called this supercontinent Pangaea, and believed that it began to separate in the late Triassic period (245 to 208 million years ago) because of a phenomenon called "continental drift."

Subsequent geologists refined the theory to distinguish between a northern landmass called Laurasia and a southern landmass called Gondwanaland, the latter which was composed of South America, Africa, peninsular India, Australia, and Antarctica.

But it wasn't until the late 1960s that the theory of plate tectonics proved Wegener correct and revolutionized geological science. Scientists think that at the center of the Earth is a huge core of liquid iron that sloshes around to create the Earth's magnetic field; above this is a thick and relatively flexible mantle covered by a thin and brittle crust (about 25 miles thick below the continents and about 6.5 miles thick below the oceans).

The crust is split into seven major and five minor plates that "float" on top of the mantle. The plates are constantly moving, pressing together, pulling apart or rubbing alongside each other at different speeds (from 1 to 4 inches per year) to form ocean ridges, mountain ranges, and volcanoes, and to cause earthquakes.

So what is the evidence that supports
continental drift? Apart from the fact that
the shapes match—the jigsaw pieces fit
together—Wegener realized that many
of the plant fossils of late Paleozoic age
found on several different continents are
similar. He was especially interested in the
similarity of plant and animal fossils on the
matching coastlines of South America and
Africa. He reasoned that they couldn't have
crossed the Atlantic ocean, so the only
other scientific explanation was that the
continents must have once been joined.

Gondwanaland

Polar Ice and Global Warming

Antarctica is a continent about one and a half times the size of the United States, which lies mostly south of the Antarctic Circle. About 98 percent of it is covered by a thick continental ice sheet thousands of feet thick, and immense glaciers form ice shelves along half of its coastline. Antarctica contains 90 percent of the ice on earth. The Arctic (the North Pole) is much smaller, but it, too, is crucial to the welfare of the planet. Most worrisome for us human inhabitants, both regions have shown signs that they are getting smaller because global warming is making them melt.

Some of the ice shelves in the northern part of the continent, known as the Antarctic Peninsula, have been collapsing over the last few years and warming of 4.5°F has been recorded since 1945. The 770-square-mile Larsen A ice shelf collapsed suddenly in 1995, and in 1998 and 1999 two more ice shelves, with a combined area of 1,150 square miles, fell into the sea. Scientists are worried that if the large West Antarctica ice sheet disintegrates, it could raise the sea level worldwide by as much as 20 feet.

In the Arctic a series of NASA studies in 2002 found that "perennial" sea ice (ice that remains all year round) is melting at a disturbing rate of 9 percent per decade. Ice also reflects the sun's light. So at both poles, the less ice there is, the less of the sun's rays are reflected, and global warming accelerates.

But scientists cannot agree on one important consequence of these global changes: whether the climate will get hotter or colder. At the moment our planet is in an interglacial period—the ice has retreated to the poles, so how could global warming lead to the next ice age?

The answer lies with the Gulf Stream, the current that takes warm water from the West Indies to the North Atlantic, without which Europe would be at least five degrees colder with bitter winters. The Gulf Stream is part of a larger system of currents called the North Atlantic Meridional Overturning Circulation (MOC), but the basic mechanism runs something like this: salty cold water in the Atlantic sinks because it is dense. As it sinks more water flows north to replace it. This thermohaline circulation (from the Greek words for heat and salt) is a crucial factor in the climate of the earth.

The problem with melting ice is that it is fresh water. When it flows into the Atlantic, it makes the ocean less salty and therefore less dense, so the flow would sink less rapidly, and the Gulf Stream would slow down. Samples of ice (ice cores) show evidence of dramatic climate changes in the past and that the thermohaline circulation could have been responsible.

One thing is certain: the climate is changing, and in ways that may not have been experienced in several million years.

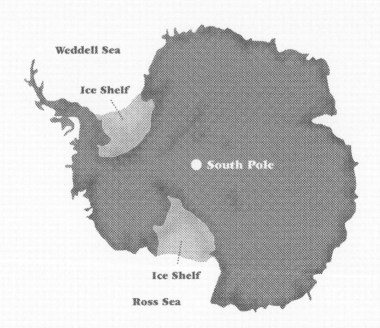

Southern Ocean

Weddell Sea

Ice Shelf

● South Pole

Ice Shelf

Ross Sea

Volcanoes: How Do They Work?

Deep inside the earth, between the molten iron core and the thin crust at the surface, there is a solid body of rock called the mantle. The mantle is subject to extremely high temperature and pressure that causes the rock to melt and become liquid (magma). It then rises up to the earth's surface and usually erupts (as lava) in areas where Earth's shifting plates meet or split apart (plate boundaries).

There are roughly three basic volcano shapes and six types of eruptions.

Types of Shapes:
1. Stratovolcanoes are usually very high with pointy tops and usually occur where plate boundaries are converging. They erupt very infrequently, but with devastating results. Mount Vesuvius, which buried the Roman city of Pompeii in A.D. 79, is a stratovolcano.

2. Shield-type volcanoes are usually spread out over a large area and are formed by plates moving over hotspots, often creating an island chain. They have gently sloping sides and frequent, small-scale eruptions. Most of the major volcanoes in Hawaii are shield volcanoes.

3. Scoria cones are the most common volcano type, usually caused by Strombolian eruptions. They are shaped like upside-down cones, with slightly squished tops. Scoria cones usually erupt only once.

Types of Eruptions:
1. Plinian
With thick lava and high gas content, they can shoot rocks, ash, and gas high into the air at high speed and last for days.

2. Hawaiian
These eruptions don't explode, but produce streams of slow-moving lava and often spew fountains of lava into the air. They last up to a few hours.

3. Strombolian

They create lots of noisy fireworks but are not very dangerous. Lava is shot skyward up to a few hundred feet, but there isn't much lava flow.

4. Vulcanian

These eruptions do not produce much lava flow either, but they tend to be larger than Strombolian ones. They produce lots of ash and chuck out volcanic rocks.

5. Hydrovolcanic

These occur when water vapor hits hot magma to form huge steam clouds.

6. Fissure

They occur where magma leaks through a long fissure in the ground to make a spectacular "curtain of fire" effect.

What Is the Difference between Active, Dormant, and Extinct Volcanoes?

An active volcano is one that has erupted sometime during the last few hundred years.

A dormant volcano is one that has not erupted during the last few hundred years, but has erupted during the last several thousand years.

An extinct volcano is one that has not erupted during the last several thousand years.

There are about 800 active or dormant volcanoes in the world.

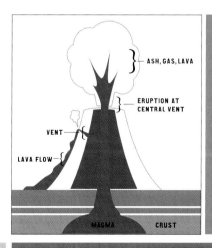

Capital Cities

How many state capitals can you name, and do you know when they entered the Union?

Montgomery, Alabama (1819)
Juneau, Alaska (1959)
Phoenix, Arizona (1912)
Little Rock, Arkansas (1836)
Sacramento, California (1850)
Denver, Colorado (1876)
Hartford, Connecticut (1788)
Dover, Delaware (1787)
Tallahassee, Florida (1845)
Atlanta, Georgia (1788)
Honolulu, Hawaii (1959)
Boise, Idaho (1890)
Springfield, Illinois (1818)
Indianapolis, Indiana (1816)
Des Moines, Iowa (1846)
Topeka, Kansas (1861)
Frankfort, Kentucky (1792)
Baton Rouge, Louisiana (1812)
Augusta, Maine (1820)
Annapolis, Maryland (1788)
Boston, Massachusetts (1788)
Lansing, Michigan (1837)
St. Paul, Minnesota (1858)
Jackson, Mississippi (1817)
Jefferson City, Missouri (1821)

Helena, Montana (1889)
Lincoln, Nebraska (1867)
Carson City, Nevada (1864)
Concord, New Hampshire (1788)
Trenton, New Jersey (1787)
Santa Fe, New Mexico (1912)
Albany, New York (1788)
Raleigh, North Carolina (1789)
Bismarck, North Dakota (1889)
Columbus, Ohio (1803)
Oklahoma City, Oklahoma (1907)
Salem, Oregon (1859)
Harrisburg, Pennsylvania (1787)
Providence, Rhode Island (1790)
Columbia, South Carolina (1788)
Pierre, South Dakota (1889)
Nashville, Tennessee (1796)
Austin, Texas (1845)
Salt Lake City, Utah (1896)
Montpelier, Vermont (1791)
Richmond, Virginia (1788)
Olympia, Washington (1889)
Charleston, West Virginia (1863)
Madison, Wisconsin (1848)
Cheyenne, Wyoming (1890)

World Capitals

Afghanistan: Kabul
Albania: Tirana
Algeria: Algiers
Andorra: Andorra la Vella
Angola: Luanda
Antigua and Barbuda: St. John's
Argentina: Buenos Aires
Armenia: Yerevan
Australia: Canberra
Austria: Vienna
Azerbaijan: Baku
Bahamas: Nassau
Bahrain: Manama
Bangladesh: Dhaka
Barbados: Bridgetown
Belarus: Minsk
Belau: Koror
Belgium: Brussels
Belize: Belmopan
Benin: Porto Novo
Bhutan: Thimphu
Bolivia: Sucre
Bosnia and Hercegovina: Sarajevo
Botswana: Gaborone
Brazil: Brasília

Brunei: Bandar Seri Begawan
Bulgaria: Sofia
Burkina Faso: Ouagadougou
Burma: Rangoon
Burundi: Bujumbura
Cambodia: Phnom Penh
Cameroon: Yaoundé
Canada: Ottawa
Cape Verde: Praia
Central African Republic: Bangui
Chad: N'djamena
Chile: Santiago
China: Beijing
Colombia: Bogotá
Comoros: Moroni
Congo, Republic of: Brazzaville
Congo, The Democratic Republic of the: Kinshasa
Costa Rica: San José
Côte d'Ivoire: Yamoussoukro
Croatia: Zagreb
Cuba: Havana
Cyprus: Nicosia
Czech Republic: Prague
Denmark: Copenhagen
Djibouti: Djibouti
Dominica: Roseau

Dominican Republic: Santo Domingo
East Timor: Dili
Ecuador: Quito
Egypt: Cairo
El Salvador: San Salvador
Equatorial Guinea: Malabo
Eritrea: Asmara
Estonia: Tallinn
Ethiopia: Addis Ababa
Fiji: Suva
Finland: Helsinki
France: Paris
Gabon: Libreville
The Gambia: Banjul
Georgia: Tbilisi
Germany: Berlin
Ghana: Accra
Greece: Athens
Grenada: St. George's
Guatemala: Guatemala City

Guinea: Conakry
Guinea-Bissau: Bissau
Guyana: Georgetown
Haiti: Port-au-Prince
Honduras: Tegucigalpa
Hungary: Budapest
Iceland: Reykjavik
India: New Delhi
Indonesia: Jakarta
Iran: Tehran
Iraq: Baghdad
Ireland, Republic of: Dublin
Israel: Jerusalem
Italy: Rome
Jamaica: Kingston
Japan: Tokyo
Jordan: Amman
Kazakhstan: Astana
Kenya: Nairobi
Kiribati: Bairiki

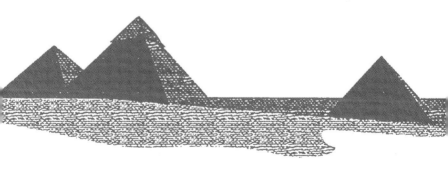

North Korea: P'yŏngyang

South Korea: Seoul

Kuwait: Kuwait City

Kyrgyzstan: Bishkek

Laos: Vientiane

Latvia: Riga

Lebanon: Beirut

Lesotho: Maseru

Liberia: Monrovia

Libya: Tripoli

Liechtenstein: Vaduz

Lithuania: Vilnius

Luxembourg: Luxembourg

Macedonia: Skopje

Madagascar: Antananarivo

Malawi: Lilongwe

Malaysia: Kuala Lumpur

Maldives: Malé

Mali: Bamako

Malta: Valletta

Marshall Islands: Majuro

Mauritania: Nouakchott

Mauritius: Port Louis

Mexico: Mexico City

Micronesia: Palikir

Moldova: Kishinev

Monaco: Monaco-Ville

Mongolia: Ulan Bator

Morocco: Rabat

Mozambique: Maputo

Namibia: Windhoek

Nauru: Yaren District

Nepal: Kathmandu

Netherlands: Amsterdam

New Zealand: Wellington

Nicaragua: Managua

Niger: Niamey

Nigeria: Abuja

Norway: Oslo

Oman: Muscat

Pakistan: Islamabad

Panama: Panama City

Papua New Guinea: Port Moresby

Paraguay: Asunción

Peru: Lima

The Philippines: Manila

Poland: Warsaw

Portugal: Lisbon

Qatar: Doha

Romania: Bucharest

Russia: Moscow

Rwanda: Kigali

St. Kitts-Nevis: Basseterre

St. Lucia: Castries

St. Vincent and the Grenadines: Kingstown

San Marino: San Marino

São Tomé and Príncipe: São Tomé

Saudi Arabia: Riyadh

Senegal: Dakar

Serbia and Montenegro: Belgrade

Seychelles: Victoria
Sierra Leone: Freetown
Singapore: Singapore City
Slovakia: Bratislava
Slovenia: Ljubljana
Solomon Islands: Honiara
Somalia: Mogadishu
South Africa: Pretoria
Spain: Madrid
Sri Lanka: Colombo
Sudan: Khartoum
Suriname: Paramaribo
Swaziland: Mbabane
Sweden: Stockholm
Switzerland: Bern
Syria: Damascus
Taiwan: Taipei
Tajikistan: Dushanbe
Tanzania: Dodoma
Thailand: Bangkok
Togo: Lomé
Tonga: Nuku'alofa
Trinidad and Tobago: Port-of-Spain
Tunisia: Tunis
Turkey: Ankara
Turkmenistan: Ashkhabad
Tuvalu: Funafuti

Uganda: Kampala
Ukraine: Kiev
United Arab Emirates: Abu Dhabi
United Kingdom: London
United States: Washington, DC
Uruguay: Montevideo
Uzbekistan: Tashkent
Vanuatu: Port Vila
Venezuela: Caracas
Vietnam: Hanoi
Western Samoa: Apia
Yemen: Sanaá
Zambia: Lusaka
Zimbabwe: Harare

Cloud Formation

*I bring fresh showers for the thirsting
   flowers,*

From the seas and the streams;

*I bear light shade for the leaves when laid
   In their noonday dreams.*

*From my wings are shaken the dews that
   wake*

The sweet buds every one,

*When rocked to rest on their mother's
   breast,*

As she dances about the sun.

—Percy Bysshe Shelley, "The Cloud"

Whether you are a Romantic poet or a meteorologist, all the clouds that you will ever see are a combination of or variation on three basic types: cumulus, stratus, and cirrus.

Cumulus Clouds:

Cumulus is Latin for a "heap" or "pile." They look like mashed potatoes with flat bases and fluffy tops. They often occur in the afternoon on a sunny day.

In the morning the sky is clear blue, the sun warms the ground, and the warm ground heats the air above it. The warm air at ground level is less dense than the air above, so it starts to rise and form into a round mass. The higher it gets, the lower the pressure so the mass spreads out and gets bigger.

The air cools as it rises so it can't hold as much water vapor as it did when it was warmer, so some of the vapor condenses into liquid cloud droplets. The mass stops rising when it is the same temperature as the surrounding air; at that point enough water vapor will have condensed to make it a visible cloud.

The size of the cloud depends on how quickly the air rises and the amount of moisture in the air. Most cumulus clouds form below 6,000 feet and don't cause rain, but they can form into thunderclouds called cumulonimbus if the upward air currents are very strong.

Stratus Clouds

Stratus is Latin for "spread out." Stratus are long flat clouds that usually form at a boundary between a layer of warm moist air moving over a layer of cool air. The warm air reaches its dew point and liquid cloud droplets form. Sometimes stratus clouds are so low that they become fog. Those floating between 6,500 and 18,000 feet are called altostratus and those above 18,000 feet are cirrostratus.

Cirrus Clouds

Cirrus comes from the Latin word for a lock of hair. Cirrus clouds are thin and wispy and they only form at very high altitudes, about 20,000 feet above the earth's surface, during fair weather. They consist of ice crystals formed from the freezing of super-cooled water droplets and are so thin that sunlight can pass through them.

Cumulus Cloud

"If the Romans had been obliged to learn Latin, they would never have found time to conquer the world."

— Heinrich Heine

THE CLASSICS ▶

Socrates, Plato, and Aristotle

Socrates (c. 469–399 B.C.):

The son of a stonecutter and a midwife, Socrates is hailed by some as the greatest genius Athens has ever produced. At a time when the Sophists were making themselves rich by teaching the art of arguing, Socrates lived a more principled life, and practiced what he preached. He lived in relative poverty and charged no fees, but the Athenian youth were enraptured by his intellect and his ability to dominate anyone who would attempt to reason against him. He was a notoriously ugly man, bald and overweight with a snub nose, but his love of philosophy and wisdom made him a celebrity.

Socrates' downfall came when he was convicted by a jury of 500 of his fellow citizens of disbelief in the state's gods and of corrupting the youth. Plato reports that Socrates was indicted as "an evil-doer and curious person, searching into things under the earth and above the heavens; and making the worse appear the better cause, and teaching all this to others." He was sentenced to death, and did not propose an alternative sentence. Socrates' high-mindedness meant that he refused to break the law—democracy must prevail, even if it meant his own death, because above all he believed in being a good citizen. Later he poisoned himself in prison with hemlock. He was just too smart for his own good, although his wisdom lay in questioning everything and knowing nothing. His legacy was that he challenged his students to take nothing for granted and to think for themselves.

Plato (c. 428–c. 347 B.C.):

Plato was Socrates' most famous pupil. Socrates appears in many of Plato's numerous dialogues and his dialectic style of question-answer-question-answer forms the structure.

Socrates never gave his students answers, only questions (now called the Socratic method)—a method that encouraged his student Plato to believe that we are born with knowledge and that the purpose of education is to bring it out through dialogue and conversation. Plato's greatest work is *The Republic*, which examines fundamental principles for the conduct of human life—the nature of justice; the achievement of knowledge, education, and morality; and the difference between appearance and reality. His theory of ideas argues the existence of a higher world of absolute forms of which perceived reality is an imperfect approximation. For example, there are hundreds of different types of chairs, and we all perceive them differently, but in the world of forms, beyond the mind, exists the definitive chair, embodying total "chairness" and expressing the true form of a chair to perfection. The same is true of concepts like justice and morality—to grasp the Form, rather than the imperfect subjective version within the human mind, is to know ultimate truth and unchanging reality. He proposed that only those schooled in philosophy to attain an understanding of the Forms (the so-called "philosopher kings") should rule—a creed that has been twisted to justify totalitarian government and autocracy ever since.

Aristotle (384–322 B.C.):

Aristotle was Plato's most famous pupil and was briefly the personal tutor of Alexander the Great. He was a man of very wide learning and lectured on just about everything, from astronomy to zoology. Few of Aristotle's writings remain, but many of those of his students do. Aristotle rejected Plato's theory of ideas, arguing instead that knowledge is acquired by experience—you can't just debate in a vacuum without the experience to back up your argument. Aristotle would say that the universal chair or the essence of "chairness" can be deduced by one's detailed investigation of many chairs. He believed in close study of the actual material world rather than sitting in an ivory tower theorizing. In this respect, his technique was the forerunner of the modern scientific method.

Homer's *Iliad* and *Odyssey*

These two epic poems—the greatest works of classical Greek literature—were written more than 2,800 years ago by a blind poet.

The *Iliad*:

The *Iliad*, through the metric music of Homer's poetry, tells the story of the war between the Greeks and the Trojans caused by Paris' elopement with Helen, wife of Menelaus, king of Sparta.

The main theme is the wrath of the Greek hero Achilles and his feud with Agamemnon, king of Mycenae and leader of the Greek army. Told in 24 books, this epic vividly conveys the horrors of war: the bloodshed, the emotional toll, the heroism and humanity of men, and the machinations of the Olympian Deities (see page 115) who intervene to help their favorite humans.

The grim reality of war is always interlaced with a yearning for peace and with many poignant moments in which the human spirit struggles to triumph over the carnage and sense of alienation. In Book 6, the Greek hero Diomedes and the Trojan hero Glaucus exchange armor and refuse to fight each other after discovering that their families were friends: this is followed by a domestic scene in which Hector's baby is frightened by his father's war helmet, so Hector removes it and takes his baby in his arms before leaving for battle, despite the pleadings of his wife, Andromache.

The violence, destruction, and profound loss of war is unremitting, culminating in the tragic death of Achilles' beloved friend Patroclus and the fierce battle to recover Patroclus' dead body. The self-destructive nature of Achilles' anger is chilling and the revenge on his killer, Hector, is brutal—after slaying him, Achilles mutilates Hector's corpse by tying it behind his chariot and dragging it away. The *Iliad* ends with a brief truce to allow the burning of Hector's body on a funeral pyre.

The Greeks   vs   The Trojans

The Greeks	The Trojans
Achilles: Son of the goddess Thetis and a mortal father; the Greeks' greatest warrior.	**Aeneas:** Trojan warrior, son of Anchises
Agamemnon: King of Mycenae. Greek leader and brother of Menelaus	**Andromache:** Hector's wife
	Astyanax: Hector's baby son
Helen: Queen of Sparta, who eloped with Paris to start the war	**Hector:** Prince of Troy, older brother of Paris
Menelaus: King of Sparta, husband of Helen	**Hecuba:** Queen of Troy, King Priam's wife
Nestor: King of Pylos	**Cassandra:** Princess of Troy, Priam's daughter
Odysseus: King of Ithaca	**Paris:** Prince of Troy (who eloped with Helen, causing the war)
Patroclus: Achilles' beloved friend	**Supported by:** Apollo, Artemis, Ares, and Aphrodite
Supported by: Hera, Athena, Poseidon, Hermes, and Hephaestus	

The *Odyssey*:

This story continues that of the *Iliad*. The Trojans have been defeated (by the "Trojan" horse) and the *Odyssey* tells the story of Odysseus and the other Greeks' attempts to return home across the sea. It takes Odysseus ten long years. The poem begins with Odysseus marooned on the island of the nymph Calypso while, back home, everyone thinks he is dead and his house is overrun with suitors trying to pair off with his wife Penelope (that is, until Zeus sends two eagles to attack each other as a sign). With Hermes' help, Odysseus escapes from Calypso only to be ship-wrecked by Poseidon. Odysseus is washed ashore and befriends Princess Nausicaa of the Phaeacians, who takes him back to her palace where he tells of his adventures with the Lotus Eaters, the Cyclops, the Laestrygonians (giants who threw boulders at his ships and ate his men), Circe turning some of his remaining men into pigs, the Sirens whose sweet singing lures sailors onto the rocks, the whirlpool Charybdis, and the crashing cliffs of Scylla. The local king takes pity on Odysseus and speeds him to his homeland of Ithaca, where he awakes and kisses the ground. (This is Book 13—there are still 11 books to go.) Athena turns him into a beggar as a disguise and he goes searching for a swineherd who recounts his life story before Odysseus is reunited with his son Telemachus. After being away for 20 years, Odysseus goes home with his son and they kill the rest of the suitors. Still in disguise (his wife doesn't recognize her husband), Odysseus reveals his identity to his over-joyed and always loyal wife.

The Olympian Deities

Aphrodite (Roman name: Venus):

Goddess of love, beauty, fertility, and sexual rapture. Also the protectress of sailors. According to Hesiod, she was born out of the sea-foam that arose when Cronus castrated his father Uranus, throwing his genitals into the sea. Homer describes Aphrodite as the daughter of Zeus and Dione. Her festival is the Aphrodisiac.

Apollo (Roman name: Apollo):

God of prophecy, music (especially the lyre), medicine and healing, poetry, and dance, and the overseer of herds and flocks. Also known as the god of light, "Phoebus." The son of Zeus and Leto, he had a twin sister, Artemis.

Ares (Roman name: Mars):

God of war. Handsome, cruel, vain, and violent. Brother of Eris, the goddess of strife, and the lame god Hephaestus. He is often shown carrying a bloody spear. His throne on Olympus is upholstered with human skin. In Roman mythology he is, in some accounts, the father of Romulus and Remus, the mythical founders of Rome.

Artemis (Roman name: Diana):

Goddess of the hunt, wild animals, and childbirth. Daughter of Zeus and Leto and sister of Apollo. Often depicted wearing animal skins and carrying a bow and arrows (made by Hephaestus and the Cyclops). Also associated with Selene, the goddess of the moon.

Athena (Roman name: Minerva):

Goddess of wisdom, justice, the arts, and war. Zeus swallowed her pregnant mother Metis to overcome a prophecy that said he would be overthrown by Metis' son. When Zeus developed a splitting headache, Hephaestus (Zeus' son) cleaved his forehead with an ax and Athena sprang out fully armed.

Demeter (Roman name: Ceres):

Goddess of agriculture. She is the daughter of Cronus and Rhea and the sister of Zeus with whom she bore her daughter Persephone, who was snatched by Hades, god of the underworld. Perpetual winter descended while Demeter mourned the loss of her daughter. Finally Hades agreed to release Persephone for one-third of each year and thus the seasons were created.

Hephaestus (Roman name: Vulcan):

God of fire and crafts, hence of black-smiths. The son of Zeus and Hera (although Hephaestus was conceived by partheno-genesis—reproduction more commonly seen among insects in which an unfertil-ized egg develops into a new individual). When Hephaestus was born lame, his mother threw him from Mount Olympus (in other accounts he was maimed by his father who threw him by the foot during a marital fight). He created the first woman, Pandora (whose dowry box, when opened, filled the world with cruelty and sickness).

Hera (Roman name: Juno):

Goddess of marriage and childbirth. She was a daughter of Cronus and Rhea and first sister, then wife, of Zeus and, there-fore, was Queen of the Olympians. She restored her virginity annually by bathing in the Spring of Canathus. Portrayed as very vengeful and jealous of her husband's numerous affairs.

Hermes (Roman name: Mercury):

The messenger of the gods and conveyor of dead souls to the Underworld. He was the son of Zeus and a mountain nymph Maia. A precocious baby, he stole cattle from Apollo when he was hours old, then invented the lyre from a tortoise shell to appease him. He was a prankster and also very helpful to mortals. Often depicted carrying a caduceus—a staff of two inter-twined snakes.

Hestia (Roman name: Vesta):

Goddess of the hearth. The oldest of the Olympian deities, she was the eldest sister of Zeus and daughter of Cronus and Rhea. She vowed to remain a virgin and rejected the advances of Apollo and Poseidon. The enclosed order of Vestal Virgins was named after her.

Poseidon (Roman name: Neptune):

God of the sea, horses, and horse-racing (often adopting the form of a steed). He spent most of the time in the sea rather than on Olympus. He was the brother of Zeus and Hades. Creation had been split among them: Zeus ruled the sky, Hades the Underworld, and Poseidon the water. Poseidon was father of the hero Theseus (although mortal Aegeus claimed he was the father of Theseus).

Zeus (Roman name: Jupiter):

Supreme god of the Olympians. He was the youngest son of the Titans Cronus and Rhea. His father swallowed his brothers and sisters at birth (Poseidon, Hades, Hestia, Demeter, and Hera) but his mother hid Zeus in a cave in Crete. When he had grown up, Zeus made Cronus vomit up his siblings, who then beat Cronus and the Titans and imprisoned them in the Underworld. Zeus was the father of the heroes Perseus and Heracles (Hercules).

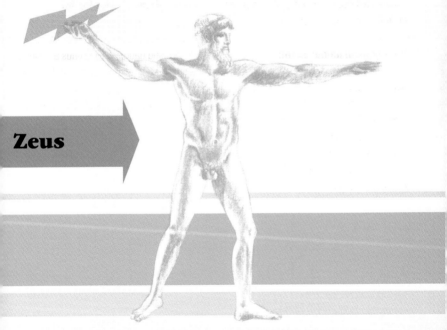

Zeus

Roman Gladiators

The Colosseum in Rome is one of the most enduring images we have of the ancient Romans' love for gladiatorial combat. But our picture of the gladiators is full of myths and inaccuracies—images of Christians being thrown to the lions (rarely), of emperors sanctioning the death of a defeated gladiator with the thumbs down signal (actually it was a thumbs up signal). So what really happened?

First it is important to note that gladiatorial games were originally associated with funerals. When an important warrior died, gladiatorial games would be offered to honor his death, and were less frequent than other forms of entertainment. The first gladiatorial games were in 264 B.C., and they quickly became popular in Rome, although they were always associated with the death of a prominent person. These games were also privately funded *(munera)* as opposed to state funded *(ludi)*, which grew popular later.

Triumph over death was the symbolic key to whole spectacle. Initially the games were held during the winter equinox and only later were they permitted during the spring equinox. The Roman mortality rate was high; many citizens died before the age of 30. The gladiators were mostly prisoners, slaves, and criminals who could win their lives or freedom if they fought well. Therefore gladiatorial games were a graphic representation of the power of men to transcend death, not merely to hasten it.

Gladiators were trained to kill and, if required, face death with dignity—both important considerations for Romans. The Romans' empire was founded upon the strength of their fighters and the prowess of individual soldiers. The games were a way of demonstrating and perpetuating this power, and the spread of gladiatorial games across the empire was a unifying force.

Gladiators were named after their place of origin (e.g., Samnite territory, Thrace) or their type of weapon.

Samnites (later called *secutor*) carried a sword and a rectangular military shield called a *scutum*, and wore a metal helmet and armor on his right arm and left leg.

Thracians used a short sword *(sica)* and a small round shield *(parma)*.

The murmillo was heavily armored with an oblong shield, a short sword, a protective visor, and fish-shaped crests on the helmet.

The retiarius had minimal armor and fought with a trident and net *(rete)*.

There were various bit players including *equites*, who fought on horseback with lances and swords; *essedarii*, who fought in chariots; and *andabatae*, who battled each other wearing helmets without eye holes. Even women gladiators later became popular during the reign of Nero. *Bestiarii* were trained to fight animals, and large numbers of the beasts were slaughtered. When Trajan became emperor, the games he hosted in celebration saw the deaths of more than 9,000 animals.

Another important part of the games was the lunchtime spectacle when *humiliores* (low-class criminals) were executed by sword, by burning at the stake, or by being delivered *ad bestias*—to hungry wild animals. This seems barbaric to modern sensibilities, but it was an important display of law and order and justice being upheld. It was only later during the reign of Nero that the spectacle descended into voyeurism—plays would be performed in which the condemned person would take a role of a character who would die—an early form of snuff movie.

Ten Greek Myths

Daedalus and Icarus:

Daedalus fled from Athens with his son Icarus after killing his nephew Talos. The duo traveled to Crete, where they were welcomed by King Minos. Daedalus built the labyrinth for the Minotaur (see "Theseus and the Minotaur" below), but Minos imprisoned them because they knew its secret. They planned their escape by building wings, but Daedalus warned his son not to fly too close to the sun. Icarus ignored his father's advice, the sun's heat melted the wax that held the feathers in place, and he plunged to his death in a part of the Aegean sea that is now known as the Icarian Sea.

Jason and the Golden Fleece:

Phrixus and Helle were the children of the King of Iolcus. Their wicked stepmother plotted against them and duped the king into thinking the Oracle had instructed him to sacrifice his children to end a long drought. Upset but resolved, the king led Phrixus and Helle to the sacrificial altar, but at the last minute a flying golden ram (a gift from Hermes) rescued them. The children climbed onto the ram's back and flew far away. Helle became so exhausted she fell to her death (in the sea now called the Hellespont), so only Phrixus survived. After delivering him safely to Colchis, the ram died and the people honored the beast by stripping its fleece and hanging it on a tree, guarded by a dragon. Meanwhile, Jason, the rightful prince of Iolcus, was sent by his uncle, who had stolen Jason's throne, on an apparently impossible quest to get the fleece. With the help of the gods, his ship the Argo, and his crew of Argonauts, Jason succeeded and returned home to claim his throne.

The Labors of Heracles (Hercules):

He was a mortal, the son of a mortal woman named Alcmene and Zeus, who gave him superhuman strength. Zeus' jealous wife Hera sent two snakes to kill the baby Heracles but he strangled them in his cot. When he was a grown man, Hera plotted against him again by sending him into a fit of madness during which he killed his wife and three children. The devastated Heracles visited the Oracle at Delphi and was assigned twelve labors in atonement. He killed the lion of Nemea, caught the Golden Hind of Ceryneia, killed the nine-headed Hydra, captured the wild boar of Mount Erymanthus, killed the Stymphalian man-eating birds, cleaned King Augeas'

revolting stables, captured the wild bull
of Crete, tamed the flesh-eating mares
of Diomedes, brought back the golden
girdle of Hippolyta, Queen of the Amazons,
brought back the chestnut cattle from the
giant Geryon, fetched the golden apples of
the Hesperides, and finally, captured Cerberus, the three-headed dog that guarded
Hades. After completing his labors,
Heracles had many other adventures, and
at his death, he became an immortal on
Mount Olympus.

Midas and the Golden Touch:
King Midas of Lydia loved collecting gold.
As a reward for his hospitality to a friend,
Dionysus granted him a wish. Midas asked
for the golden touch. Dionysus granted the
wish but warned him against greed. At first
Midas was very happy, but soon everything he touched turned to gold—even his
servants, his food, and his children. Midas
realized his folly and begged Dionysus
to retract the wish. Dionysus told him to
bathe in the river Pactolus, after which Midas took a jug of water back to his palace
and washed everything back to normal.

Cerberus

Narcissus:

Narcissus was a beautiful young man with whom many young women fell in love, including a nymph called Echo. As punishment for upsetting Hera, the queen of the gods, Echo could only repeat the last three words of whomever she was talking to. So she was unable to tell Narcissus of her love. When she spoke, he teased her until she ran away crying. Echo withered away into just a voice and Aphrodite punished Narcissus by allowing him to fall in love with his own reflection in a pool of water. He didn't know he was bewitched by his own reflection, and every time he touched the water, the image disappeared. He pined away for his "lost love," his looks deteriorated, and he died. The gods made a flower—the narcissus—grow in his place.

Orpheus and Eurydice:

Orpheus was a musician who married a nymph called Eurydice. She trod on a poisonous snake, died, and went to the Underworld. Orpheus was so sad that he visited the underworld and begged for her return. Orpheus charmed the souls of Hades with his lyre until he relented. Eurydice was allowed to follow him out of Hades, so long as he didn't turn around to check if she was there. They almost reached safety when Orpheus looked back and Eurydice was drawn back to Hades. His lack of trust lost her forever.

Pandora's Box:

Pandora was the first mortal woman, created out of clay by Hephaestus. Athena breathed life into her, Aphrodite made her beautiful, and Hermes taught her to be beguiling. Zeus then sent her as a gift to Prometheus' brother, Epimetheus, in revenge for being tricked earlier by Prometheus. Epimetheus fell in love with her and when they married, Zeus gave Pandora a wedding gift of a beautiful box, which he instructed her never to open. Pandora or Epimetheus succumbed to curiosity and peeked inside and released suffering into the world—disease, greed, old age, death, cruelty, and war. Only hope remained in the now empty box.

Perseus and Medusa:

Perseus lived with his mother Danaë on the island of Seriphus. The tyrant king Polydectes wanted to marry Danaë, but she refused. In revenge, the king sent Perseus to kill Medusa, knowing he wouldn't return alive, since all who looked on her and her hair made of snakes were turned to stone. However, the gods helped Perseus in his quest; Athena gave him a shiny shield and Hermes gave him a sharp sword. Perseus then visited the Graiae, three hags who shared one tooth and one eye. He stole the eye and made the hags tell him where to find Medusa. On his way there, he passed through the land of Nymphs and was given a cap of invisibility, a shoe of swiftness to escape, and a special bag for Medusa's head. Using the shield to view Medusa's reflection, Perseus beheaded her. He took the head back to Seriphus and rescued his mother by showing Medusa's head to everyone in the king's court, thus turning them to stone.

edusa

Theseus and the Minotaur:

During a power struggle with his brothers for the throne of Crete, Minos prayed to Poseidon to send him a magnificent white bull as a sign of approval. He promised to sacrifice the bull, but when he saw it, he kept it for himself and sacrificed the best of his own herd. When Poseidon found out, he made Minos' wife Pasiphae fall in love with the bull and the resulting offspring was the Minotaur, a monster with the head and tail of a bull and the body of a man.

Minos imprisoned the Minotaur in a gigantic labyrinth, and each year for nine years, seven young men and women were sent from Athens as food. Theseus volunteered to be one of the human sacrifices, but when he arrived at Crete, Minos' daughter Ariadne fell in love with him. She gave him a ball of thread, which he fastened to the entrance of the maze then unravelled as he journeyed into the center, where he found and killed the Minotaur. Then Theseus retraced his steps back to his love by following the thread.

The Trojan Horse:

The Trojan War was caused when Prince Paris abducted Helen, queen of Sparta. The Greek warriors set sail for Troy to bring her back and the war waged for ten years, with heavy losses on both sides. Finally Athena, the goddess of war, gave Odysseus a plan. The Greeks built a huge wooden horse and left it in their camp, then pretended to sail away. The Trojans discovered their abandoned camp and the wooden horse. After much debate they dragged it into the city of Troy and had a big party to celebrate the end of the war. That night, Greek warriors, who had been hiding in the hollow horse, climbed out of a trap door and slaughtered the Trojan troops while they slept. They rescued Helen and sailed home.

"Too many pieces of music
finish too long after the end."

— Igor Stravinsky

MUSIC ▶

Why Are There Twelve Notes in a Musical Scale?

You may already know that a musical scale is made up of 12 notes. On the piano, each octave (the interval between any two frequencies having the ratio of 1:2) of 12 is made up of seven "white" notes labeled A through G and five "black" notes. But why are there 12? Why not 10 or 15 or 30? You may be surprised to learn that the 12-note scale is actually a compromise—a good one, but by no means perfect.

The pitch (or frequency) of a note is measured in cycles per second; for example, A above middle C is 440 cycles per second. The distance between two notes is called an interval, and it is measured as the ratio of their pitches. Notes sound pleasantly harmonic if the ratio can be expressed in small integers; otherwise they will sound dissonant. For example, the ratio for the octave is 2/1; the perfect fifth is 3/2; the perfect fourth is 4/3; the major third is 5/4; the minor third is 6/5; the major sixth is 5/3; and the minor sixth is 8/5—all small integers.

By dividing the octave into 12 exactly equal intervals (semitones), the modern equal temperament system was born. The semitone is not a simple integer ratio but is the twelfth root of two that equals approximately 1.059. This means that none of the intervals except the octave are perfect, but they are very close, to within 1 percent. Scales that use more than 12 notes would have some very pure intervals, but a good many dissonant ones too. Using 12 intervals is the only system that produces nearly perfect ratios.

But the 12 notes still need to be combined in the right way to be tonal and harmonic (if that's what you prefer, and most people do). In the early twentieth century, Arnold Schoenberg devised a system, called 12-tone technique, using all 12 chromatic notes of the scale in existing arrangements, denying a tonal center and giving each equal importance to create his atonal music. Many greeted his music with contempt, but supporters saw it and the 12-tone music of other composers, such as Berg and Webern, as the "emancipation of dissonance."

| 1 | 2 | 3 | 4 | 5 | 6 | | 8 | 9 | 10 | | 12 | | | 15 |
| F | E | C | F | A | C | | F | G | A | | C | | | E |

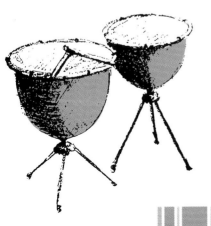

The Orchestra

The word orchestra originally referred to the area in front of the stage in an ancient Greek amphitheater that was used by the chorus to sing and dance. Groups of musicians have gathered together to play since the time of the ancient Egyptians, but modern orchestras began in the late sixteenth century when composers started to write music for instrumental groups and use "orchestration" (specifying what instrument should play which part). One of the first example's of this appears in Giovanni Gabrieli's *Sacrae Symphoniae* (1597). Monteverdi's *Orfeo* (1607) was the first opera to employ a large group of instruments and assign specific parts to each one.

There are four groups of musical instruments: strings, woodwind, brass, and percussion. Since the seventeenth century the core has been the string section, which contains about 50 percent of the musicians. A typical orchestra would have 20 first violins, 18 to 20 second violins, 14 violas, 12 cellos, and eight double basses. The brass and woodwind sections each forms about 20 percent, and the percussion about 10 percent.

Unlike the strings, where several musicians play the same musical parts, the woodwind and brass sections usually have only one player per part. A typical woodwind section will have three oboes, bassoons, clarinets, English horns, and flutes, with players doubling up on the double bassoon, bass clarinet, or piccolo.

The brass section often includes four French horns, three trumpets, three trombones, and a tuba. Finally the percussion section has just one or two players plus a timpani section (kettle drums), harp, and piano, although many more modern pieces require much larger percussion sections.

The brass instruments became standard during the eighteenth century and came into their own with the works of Beethoven and the invention of the valve in about 1815, which made the horn and trumpet completely chromatic. It wasn't until the late eighteenth century that all the woodwinds became established orchestra members, although today they are important to add subtle color to the string sound and sometimes to carry the melody, while the brass instruments are the "big guns" that create sharp dynamics.

The seating of the orchestra is specified by the conductor, but usually the first and second violins sit at the front on the conductor's left; the violas, cellos, and basses at the front right; woodwind and brass are directly in front of the conductor, behind the strings; and the percussion is at the back.

Thirty Classical Composers and Their Greatest Works

Here are 30 of the most celebrated classical composers and three recommended tasters to introduce you to their music.

Henry Purcell (1659–1695):
Ode to St. Cecelia, Dido and Aeneas, The Fairy Queen

Antonio Vivaldi (1678–1741):
The Four Seasons, Gloria in D major, Flute Concerto Op. 10, La Notte

Johann Sebastian Bach (1685–1750):
Toccata and Fugue in D minor, Brandenburg Concertos, Mass in B minor

George Frideric Handel (1685–1759):
Messiah, Music for the Royal Fireworks, "Arrival of the Queen of Sheba"

Franz Josef Haydn (1732–1809):
Symphony No. 101 ("The Clock"), Trumpet Concerto in E flat, Piano Sonata No. 58

Wolfgang Amadeus Mozart (1756–1791):
Symphony No. 40, Piano Concerto No. 21, Requiem

Ludwig van Beethoven (1770–1827):
Symphony No. 5, Piano Sonata No. 14 ("Moonlight"), Violin Sonata No. 5 ("Spring")

Gioacchino Rossini (1792–1868):
William Tell, The Barber of Seville, The Thieving Magpie

Franz Schubert (1797–1828):
Symphony No. 8 ("Unfinished"), Impromptu No. 3 in G flat, Quintet for Piano and Strings ("Trout")

Felix Mendelssohn (1809–1847):
Symphony No. 4 ("Italian"), Violin Concerto in E minor, *The Hebrides* overture

Frédéric Chopin (1810–1849):
Nocturne No. 2 in E flat, Fantasie Impromptu in C sharp minor, Etudes Op. 10

Robert Schumann (1810–1856):
Symphony No. 4, Piano Concerto, *Scenes of Childhood* Op. 15

Franz Liszt (1811–1886):
Piano Concerto No. 2, Hungarian Rhapsody No. 2, Liebesträume

Richard Wagner (1813–1883):
Tannhäuser, Tristan und Isolde, Der Ring des Nibelungen

Giuseppe Verdi (1813–1901):
Aïda, Requiem, *Rigoletto*

Johannes Brahms (1833–1897):
Piano Concerto No. 2, Symphony No. 1,
Hungarian Dance No. 5

Peter Ilych Tchaikovsky (1840–1893):
Fantasy Overture *(Romeo and Juliet)*, Symphony No. 6 ("Pathétique"), *Swan Lake*

Antonin Dvořák (1841–1904):
Symphony No. 9 ("From the New World"),
Cello Concerto No. 2 in B minor, Serenade for
Strings in E major

Edvard Grieg (1843–1907):
Peer Gynt, Piano Concerto in A minor,
String Quartet in G Minor

Edward Elgar (1857–1934):
Enigma Variations, Cello Concerto,
Violin Concerto

Giacomo Puccini (1858–1924):
Turandot, Madam Butterfly, Tosca

Gustav Mahler (1860–1911):
Symphony Nos. 4 and 5,
Kindertotenlieder, Funeral March

Claude Debussy (1862–1918):
Prélude à l'après-midi d'un faune,
Nocturnes, *Chansons de Bilitis*

Richard Strauss (1864–1949):
Also Sprach Zarathustra,
Der Rosenkavalier, Don Juan

Jean Sibelius (1865–1957):
Finlandia, Violin Concerto, Symphonies
Nos. 2 and 5

Ralph Vaughan Williams (1872–1958):
Symphony No. 2 (A London Symphony), *The*
Lark Ascending, Fantasia on a Theme by
Thomas Tallis

Sergei Rachmaninov (1873–1943):
Piano Concertos Nos. 2 and 3, *Rhapsody on*
a Theme of Paganini, Piano Preludes

Igor Stravinsky (1882–1971):
The Rite of Spring, The Firebird,
Symphony of Psalms

Sergei Prokofiev (1891–1953):
Romeo and Juliet, Piano Concerto No. 3,
Violin Concerto No. 1

Benjamin Britten (1913–1976):
Peter Grimes, String Quartet No. 3,
Cello Symphony

Musical Notation

If you look at a piece of music, there's a good chance you'll see lots of words peppered around above the score, usually in Italian (but sometimes in German or French). Many of them are instructions relating to the tempo, or speed at which a piece is to be played. During the Renaissance, Italy was the center of musical learning, and musicians traveled from all over the world to study at the musical hub of Europe, and then took the Italian notations back home. That is why the Italian system is still so widely used.

There are hundreds of these instructions, but here are some of the most common:

a tempo: return to a previous tempo

accelerando, accel: getting steadily faster

adiagietto: slow (but faster than adagio)

adagio: slow (but faster than largo), also thoughtful

allegretto: pretty lively

allegro: quick, lively, and bright

andante: "moving along," medium pace (walking pace)

andantino: a little faster than andante

cantabile: "singable," a singing, lyrical style

con moto: with movement, or a certain quickness

da capo, D.C.: repeat the piece from the beginning to the end or to a place marked *fine*

dioppio movimento: twice as fast

dolce: sweet

grave: very slow and solemn

largamente: broadly

larghetto: less slow than largo

larghissimo: as slow as possible

largo: very slow and dignified

legato: play without any perceptible interruption between the notes

lentamente: slowly

lento: slow

licenza: "licence," freedom—be free with the style

lunga pausa: a long pause

martellato: "hammered," percussive

moderato: moderate tempo between andante and allegro

pizzicato: play by plucking the strings

prestissimo: as quickly as possible

presto: fast

rallentando, rall.: getting gradually slower

rapido: rapid

ritardando, rit., ritard.: getting gradually slower

ritenuto, rit. or riten.: holding back tempo

tempo primo: returning to tempo at beginning

veloce: speedily

vivace: quick and lively

Ten Operas Explained

Turandot, Giacomo Puccini:

In Ancient Peking, the suitors of Princess Turandot must answer three riddles correctly or die. At the execution of the latest doomed suitor, a slave girl, Liù, calls for help when her old master is knocked down in the crowd. A handsome youth, Prince Calàf, recognizes him as his long-lost father Timur. Liu's love for Calàf has kept her loyal to the old man. When Calàf sees Princess Turandot's beauty, he takes up the challenge despite ministers Ping, Pang, and Pong's attempts to discourage him. He answers the riddles correctly then challenges Turandot that if she discovers his name by dawn, she may yet kill him. Turandot decrees that no one in Peking shall sleep until the stranger's name is discovered. Liù stabs herself to protect his identity and by dawn Calàf kisses the ice queen, melts her heart, and she announces that his name is Love.

The Barber of Seville, Gioachino Rossini:

Seville, 1800s. Count Almaviva serenades Rosina, who is kept in her house by her jealous guardian, Dr. Bartolo. The barber, Figaro, arrives and sings his own praises, then agrees to help Almaviva win Rosina. Dr. Bartolo and Don Basilio, the music master, plot to discredit Almaviva. Figaro overhears them and agrees to deliver a note from Rosina to Almaviva, who then disguises himself as a drunken soldier to pass her a love note in reply. Then he disguises himself as a substitute music teacher, since Don Basilio is "ill." When Don Basilio turns up in good health, Almaviva bribes him to play along. An official arrives to marry Rosina to Dr. Bartolo, but he weds the two young lovers before Bartolo arrives.

Tosca, Giacomo Puccini:

Cesare Angelotti, an escaped political prisoner, hides in a church where his painter friend, Mario Cavaradossi, is working on his portrait of Mary Magdalene. Angelotti reveals himself to his friend Mario, then hides again when Mario's jealous girlfriend Tosca arrives. Baron Scarpia, the head of the secret police, is on Angelotti's trail and takes sadistic pleasure in making Tosca think that Mario has been unfaithful. Mario is captured and tortured, but he refuses to reveal the whereabouts of Angelotti. When Tosca spills the beans, Mario is dragged off to prison; then Scarpia offers to free him if she will sleep with him. She agrees and the baron orders a mock execution, but as soon as he has written a safe-conduct for them, Tosca stabs him. The execution turns out to be real. Mario is shot and Tosca leaps to her death.

The Marriage of Figaro, Wolfgang Amadeus Mozart:

A country estate outside Seville, late eighteenth century. Figaro and the maid Susanna plan to wed, but his master, Count Almaviva, fancies her too. A scheming gentleman called Bartolo wants Figaro to marry his housekeeper, Marcellina, to cancel a debt. The horny page Cherubino arrives, but hides when the count appears. The Count pursues Susanna, then hides when the music master Don Basilio arrives. Cherubino has a crush on the countess and agrees to her plan to dress him up as Susanna in order to trick the count.

Unexpectedly, the count arrives, so Cherubino hides in the closet. The count fetches a crowbar to open the locked closet, but when he returns, the real Susanna has swapped places and Cherubino has escaped through the window. After the gardener storms in, complaining about crushed geraniums under the widow, Figaro pretends it was he who had jumped. The wedding is delayed by a court summons. Meanwhile, Susanna leads the count on with a promise of a rendezvous in the garden. Figaro and Marcellina embrace after they discover that they are mother and son, which Susanna sees and misinterprets as an amorous liaison until she learns the truth. Figaro and Susanna are finally married. That evening there are many shenanigans in the garden involving love letters, a hat pin, lots of mistaken identity, and cross-dressing, culminating in Figaro and "the countess" (Susanna in disguise) being caught having sex by the count. The count apologizes for his mistake and everyone is reunited.

Don Giovanni,
Wolfgang Amadeus Mozart:

Seville, 1660s. Don Giovanni will sleep with anything in a skirt. He spends the whole opera manipulating and trying to seduce whoever strikes his fancy. He kills the commendatore, the aging local army commander, in a duel after trying to ravish his daughter, Donna Anna. He even attempts to seduce Zerlina, who is already betrothed to Masetto. An old flame, Donna Elvira, warns everyone not to trust him. Giovanni fails to seduce Zerlina and then accuses his long-suffering servant Leporello of attacking her so he can escape once again. Then he exchanges clothes with Leporello to seduce Donna Elvira's maid; Leporello almost gets beaten up by a vengeful mob that is searching for Giovanni. Meanwhile, Don Giovanni encounters the talking statue of the commendatore and invites it to dinner. Donna Elvira fails to get him to atone for his sins. When the statue arrives, Giovanni's house goes up in flames and he suffers the torments of hell for being so wicked.

Madame Butterfly, **Giacomo Puccini:**

Japan, early twentieth century. United States Navy Lieutenant B. F. Pinkerton marries a young geisha girl, Cio-Cio-San (Madame Butterfly), but he doesn't intend to keep his vows, while she takes them more seriously. Her uncle, a Buddhist priest, denounces the marriage and her for rejecting her religion. Fast forward three years; Cio-Cio-San is waiting for her husband to return from his naval adventures. She is almost penniless, but rejects a wealthy suitor; she has a child Dolore (Trouble), and remains faithful to her husband. He does finally return, but with his new American wife Kate. Cio-Cio-San sends her son into the garden to play, then stabs herself.

Carmen, Georges Bizet

Seville: Spain, early nineteenth century. The sexy and passionate Spanish gypsy Carmen is attracted to the soldier Don José, but she is bad news. He ends up saving her from prison, deserting his platoon, and joining a band of smugglers for her. But their love is destructive. When he returns from his mother's deathbed, he finds Carmen with the bull fighter Escamillo, with whom she has begun an affair. José confronts her and pleads for her to come back to him, but she refuses to be tamed, so he stabs her.

La Traviata, Giuseppe Verdi:

Frail party chick Violetta Valéry abandons her hedonistic lifestyle to settle down with Alfredo Germont. They move to the country and are blissfully happy until one day, while Alfredo is away his father arrives and tells her that her association with his son has destroyed their family's reputation and fortunes. Heartbroken, she leaves her lover, pretending she wants to return to her former life. That evening at a party in Paris, Alfredo denounces her and is challenged to a duel with her former admirer, Baron Douphol. Six months later, Violetta is dying from tuberculosis when Alfredo arrives to beg her forgiveness. They plan to leave the city forever, but the illness claims Violetta at last and she falls dead at her lover's feet.

Aïda, Giuseppe Verdi:

Memphis, ancient Egypt. The young officer Radamès loves Aïda, the Ethiopian slave of Egyptian Princess Amneris. Unfortunately, both women love him. Aïda is torn between her love for him and her homeland because she is a princess, the daughter of Amonasro, king of Ethiopia. Radamès is chosen to command the army against the advancing Ethiopians. They are defeated and Radamès returns triumphant. One of his captives is Amonasro who pleads with Aïda not to reveal his identity. He persuades his daughter to ask Radamès where the Egyptian army will enter Ethiopia. Radamès' love for Aïda makes him betray his country and, when he refuses to marry Amneris, she sentences him to death. He is buried alive in a crypt where he is joined by Aïda who has hidden there so they can die together.

La Bohème, Giacomo Puccini:

Christmas Eve, Paris, 1830s. Follows the fortunes of a group of poverty-stricken young bohemians: Marcello, a painter; Rodolfo, a poet; Colline, a philosopher; and Schaunard, a musician. Rodolfo meets and falls in love with Mimi, a young neighbor in poor health. The group celebrates Christmas Eve at Café Momus where Marcello is reconciled with a former lover, Musetta. Two months later, Rodolfo and Mimi are on the rocks. Mimi is dying and Rodolfo is jealous of her flirting with other men, but is wracked with guilt about considering leaving her. They pledge to stay together until spring, while Marcello and Musetta argue and split up. Later Mimi's health deteriorates further and the friends pawn their possessions to buy medicine, but she dies. Rofolfo rushes to her side and wails her name.

Index

Index